Revolution for Nature

Revolution for Nature:
From the Environment to the Connatural World

Klaus Michael Meyer-Abich

Translated by Matthew Armstrong

The White Horse Press
Cambridge, UK

and

University of North Texas Press
Denton, USA

First English publication 1993 by The White Horse Press,
10 High Street, Knapwell, Cambridge CB3 8NR, UK

Co-published in the USA by University of North Texas Press,
PO Box 13856, Denton, Texas, USA

Set in 10/12 New Century Schoolbook
Printed and Bound in Great Britain

ISBN *USA and dependencies*:
        0-929398-70-X (cloth); 0-929398-69-6 (pbk)
ISBN *rest of the world*:
        1-874267-08-1 (cloth); 1-874267-02-2 (pbk)

For people who are doing something about it

Contents

The translator would like to thank Johannes Felber for his invaluable assistance, and Joanne Turner and Rachel Armstrong for their help in the revision process.

Foreword

The revolutions in Eastern Europe have been greeted as a triumph for western free market principles, but with what justification? The problems in our society remain unsolved. Where is our own revolution against our life-destroying economy? The truth is that that has now become more difficult in the face of what seems like political justification for our prosperity. However, the resolution of former conflicts has at least given us the opportunity to follow a new path together, rather than carrying on along the same old road.

This book considers why we continue to destroy the environment, in spite of being quite well aware of the consequences. The problem is not confined to actions, although it is true these are based on false interests; more importantly, we suffer from a false mental outlook based on distorted perceptions.

Reason itself can save us from a rationale that is anything but reasonable. I present the evidence that we belong in nature, and can develop our sense of living within nature's whole. My contention is that the long accepted opposition between nature and culture is leading us astray, and that culture should be seen as our contribution to the development of nature, in politics and economics as well as in the creative arts. A world with humans in it can be better and more beautiful than one without, provided that we respect the intrinsic value, or dignity, of all things in the connatural world within nature's whole. Our anthropocentric ethic must give way to a holistic one. We must recognize what we owe for living, on account of other beings' lives.

The natural philosophical approach has political consequences; for individuals, the first blow to a life-threatening economic system should be to withdraw economic acceptance.

Foreword

As consumers, we can do this simply by taking a non-violent stand, all together and each for the others. We shall feel impelled to do so when we stop shielding ourselves from the destruction of the natural foundations of life by numbing our senses to it.

However, this brings into question various aspects of our constitution, and even of the prevailing concept of private property. I suggest that in a future German constitution, social duties should be complemented by duties to nature. Humanity is not a closed society, and even political reason is a gift from nature. Our state should be seen not only as a social state, but rather as a state within nature – or as a natural state.

This book has a forerunner, *Ways to Peace with Nature*. The present book takes us further in the same direction. As before, peace with nature is my concern. But how can we achieve such peace, in our actions and outlook, individual and political? That question has become more pressing even than before.

Acknowledgements

I am thankful that this book could be prepared for publication at the new Institute for Cultural Studies in Nordrhein-Westfalen. Richard Hope-Sailer, Hans Werner Ingensiep, Dietrich Koch, Sibylle Schindler and Renate Schütz shared my efforts to promote our cultural awareness of nature in the environmental crisis and reacted to the text before it was finalized. In addition, I have had very helpful stimulus from Jann Meyer-Abich and Reinhard Ueberhorst. It frequently came to my mind what Zeyde-Margreth Erdmann, Michael Müller and Ilona Zucker would say. For the English edition I am indebted to Matthew Armstrong who did well in easing out unnecessary complications. Finally the publisher himself stepped into the reader's shoes, and we spent a weekend in lively discussion which helped to make my ideas clearer. My heartfelt thanks to all the above.

Chapter 1

Thinking and Acting For Change

In spite of all the current efforts to protect the environment, the conundrum which has characterized environmental politics up to now remains unsolved: *We cannot go on like this – we know what we should be doing instead – but we don't do it*.

Why don't we do it? Of course, there are conflicting economic interests. But that is not the whole problem: the question is not only who has particular interests, but also why these prevail. Political intervention is called for whenever individual interests threaten the common good.

Yet the destruction of the very conditions required for life is only being slowed down a little here and there. We are still far from turning to life by changing our way of living. All we are doing is postponing disaster to some extent. Why? The answer is that these conditions are not simply being destroyed by wrong actions; the environmental crisis is equally a crisis of awareness.

The impulse for change comes from the recognition that other living beings in the world are not only *around* us, but *with* us. Each organism requires its particular environment, its specific habitat. The human environment is one of these many different habitats, our place to live within nature's whole. Industrial society has misunderstood this so that the whole world is interpreted merely as human habitat, and we speak of a single environment, our own, which alone should be protected. As a result we have reached a crisis in our relationship with nature.

If we do not respect the particularity of other environments, other species will at best only be able to find niches within the human habitat. We fail to see their intrinsic value and the part they play in nature's whole, and behave as if they were there simply for *our* benefit. Even the concept of the environment becomes misleading if we fail to be aware of its plurality. Seen as *our* environment, the earth appears to be nothing more than a stage set with *us* at the centre. In order to escape from this misconception, which has shaped environmental politics up to now, we should see and treat everything in nature as sharing with us in the world: not as something for us and *around* us but as being *with* us. Taking the term *connaturalia* from Latin, the world with us is our connatural world. I therefore distinguish between nature as the whole and the connatural world as the non-human part of the whole.

We must be considerate not only in our dealings with people, but also in those with the connatural world. The extent of human abuses is always most apparent in the exercise of power. In ancient times treatment of slaves was a measure of humanity, as Plato emphasized in his Laws.[1] Those who treat people in their power in an inhuman fashion show their true character. For our industrial society, treatment of the environment is a corresponding measure of humanity. Until now we have shied away from this test, shielding ourselves from perceiving the destruction we cause, so that we have become incapable of recognizing the environment as alive. That is why change must start by bringing our senses back to life.

Reviving our Senses

We can learn a great deal about perceiving and interpreting the connatural world in its own terms from the environmental teaching of the behavioural scientist Jakob von Uexküll (1864-1944), the man who first introduced the concept of 'environment' into ecology. Uexküll's starting point was the difference between the sense organs of different species. The perceptions of any creature depend on what sense organs it has. This is apparent even in human beings: blind people and deaf mutes need special provision before they can live in the same sur-roundings as the rest of us. The world seen through the eyes of a cat is very different from the world seen through human eyes. Do these differences exist only because of perceptual variations between different species, such as the way bats can hear ultrasound while humans cannot? If this were so, then ulti-mately the different perceptions of various living things would apply to one and the same world.

　　Goethe put it well when he said that if the human eye were not akin to the sun we would be unable to perceive light.[2] But it must also be pointed out that the sun, seen from earth, is akin to the eye which perceives it, in our case the human eye.[3] What an eye sees depends not only upon the object viewed, but equally upon the way in which the eye is formed. What it sees, if it sees anything at all, is perceived in terms of light and colour, but the same effects can be prompted by chemicals or by a punch. Bells provide another example. To some extent the way they ring depends on the way they are struck, but they can only make the sounds which lie within them. Ultimately a bell rings according to its own physical nature. Should we not perhaps realize that the world perceived by the human eye is primarily akin to the eye, and not necessarily the way things are?

　　Immanuel Kant (1724-1804) described how we inevitably assess things in space and time in human forms of perception, and Uexküll generalized this theory by saying that other species as well live in their own worlds. Shouldn't we acknowl-edge that they are aware of the world in their own way, just as we are, and accept that each species perceives the world according to its own needs and abilities? Uexküll's most famous example is the tick. '[It] hangs motionless on the end of a branch, in a clearing of a wood or a forest. By virtue of this position it has the chance of falling on a passing mammal. It notices nothing of all that happens around it. Then a mammal actually approaches, whose blood the tick needs to produce offspring.

　　And now something wonderful happens. Of all the effects caused by the mammal's body only three stimulate the tick, and these three in a particular order. Within the immense world which surrounds the tick three things act as signals, as flashes of light in the darkness, which guide it on the way to the certain achievement of its aims.'[4]

The first signal which the tick perceives is the smell of butyric acid, present in the sweat of all mammals. It notices nothing else. While we must learn to see what is common to the great variety of mammals, to it they are all exactly the same, whether horse or donkey, man or dog, deer or mouse. Whenever it smells butyric acid it takes notice and drops from its branch. Then it comes to the second part of the process, which it can perform with the aid of a rudimentary sense of touch. It must decide whether it has landed in the fur of its victim, or on the ground. Finally, if it has landed correctly, it seeks a place where there is more warmth than on the outer surface of the fur, where it can bore into bare skin and suck the blood of its victim. If it has landed on the ground, it returns to the trees, and by means of a sense of dark and light finds its way once more to the end of a branch.

In the world of the tick there is little more than these differences – butyric acid or nothing, fur or not fur, warm or cold, and dark or light. A newspaper for ticks would not have much to report! It is equally astounding that these three perceptions of the mammal should correspond exactly with three abilities possessed by the tick, or in Uexküll's terms with three actions available to it: letting itself fall, being able to crawl, and being able to suck blood.

'The whole richness of the world which surrounds the tick collapses, and is transformed into an impoverished system, which essentially consists only of three perceptions and three actions – its whole environment. The impoverished nature of its environment conditions its behavioural certainty, and this security is more important than any abundance.'[5]

Can we still say that humans and ticks live in the same world? Our immediate conclusion is that different species live in entirely different worlds. Astonishingly, in at least a few of these cases, we can use our reasoning ability to place ourselves in their position, at least so far that from within the frame of our own boundaries we can also perceive theirs. 'In the world of the earthworm there exist only things which relate to earthworms, while in the world of the dragonfly there exist only things which relate to dragonflies'.[6] It is as if each species were a different key, and for each one nature were a different lock. We should therefore pose the question the other way around, by asking how these different worlds can link together, so that a natural community evolves, where species are yet connected to one another. But we can only approach this question when we no longer consider our own world to be the absolute world, but realize that our environment is one out of many, and that each other species similarly has its own environment. In today's crisis, this plurality is the most important aspect of Uexküll's ecological teaching.

We may sometimes get the impression that even other human beings live in a different world from our own. An example of this, which introduces another concept of decisive significance for our awareness of the connatural world, is Uexküll's meeting with a man in Naples. He was 'a man in the prime of life, who, as a result of thirty years of exhausting and tireless labour, had raised himself in a quite honest fashion from humble bank clerk to multi-millionaire. Having arrived at the peak of his riches he decided that from then on he would enjoy his life rather than thinking about business, and, as he had up to that point seen almost nothing, he wanted to travel. Where should he go? To the most beautiful place in the world – hence to Naples. When he arrived there he was terribly disappointed. There were mountains, the sea, and the sky, but he did not find anything special about them. He wanted to see something interesting, but when he went to Pompeii, he found nothing but collapsed houses. He then went to Paestum, where he found the same thing. After a few despairing efforts to find beauty, he turned to the only concrete pleasure left – alcohol. After a number of weeks he was brought back home, suffering from *delirium tremens*. His milieu had slowly degenerated during his one-sided working life.'[7] Uexküll still spoke here of milieu in the sense of the Swedish *miljö*, but two years later he introduced the concept of 'environment' into the behavioural sciences.

The man he described obviously lived in a different world from those who can enjoy Italy's beautiful landscape and cultural wonders. He was blind in sight and insight, but most of all in receptivity to experience, which involves both of these. Yet he would presumably have been able to show himself superior to most connoisseurs and experts in the art of living in his assessment of investment risks.

Almost everyone has similar, if less extreme, examples of the way people live in their own worlds. I mention this story because it reminds me that in Central Europe in the twentieth century, and more particularly in the decades since the Second World War, half the native plant and animal species of the area have died out or are threatened with extinction – without industrial society even noticing. Plants and animals disappear in silence because they can no longer endure our way of life, and cannot find their own world within an environment we see simply as our own. This is terrible enough, but how can we tolerate the fact that we have not even noticed what we did to them?

Does Uexküll's story of the man in Naples who was blind to experience help us in understanding the blindness of today's society towards the extinction of species? The degeneration of his environment (his 'milieu'), as a consequence of the one-sidedness of his working life over many years, exemplifies another central point in Uexküll's environmental teaching, as important as the pluralism of the environment, namely the interlinkage between the worlds of action and perception. In Uexküll's understanding, environments are pragmatic contexts in the sense of the Greek word *prágma*: i.e. that which one has something to do with. As he later expressed it, the world of perception and the world of action fit together like the two halves of a zip. This is also true of human actions in the environmental crisis, which correspond to an equally topsy-turvy world of perception. Admittedly, in the case of humans, this world is not simply one of impressions gained from the senses; but rather one in which sight and insight – sensory experience and thought – are combined in a way specific to us.

'...an animal can perform as many actions as it can

distinguish objects in its environment.'⁸ Thus 'a simple animal is surrounded by a simple environment, while an animal whose abilities are more varied has an environment which is equally richly structured.' The world of a cat is at once what it observes and what it can do, but the same is also valid for a tick. Uexküll names these interlinkages between perception and action 'spheres of functioning'. For each species there are several spheres of this kind, defined by how what a living being perceives fits with its actions, for example the sphere of its prey, the sexual sphere and the sphere of its enemies.

We might remember that the concept of perception once had a much broader meaning than that of simple observation, including how a perceived opportunity or responsibility indicates a corresponding course of action. Uexküll's environments show themselves to be worlds of perception in this wider sense. In another telling example, he showed how the ability to distinguish is linked to life's actions, or, in a more general sense, how knowledge and interest are interlinked in perception. A dog 'was trained at the command "chair" to jump on a chair which stood before him. Then the chair was taken away, and the command repeated. It became clear that the dog treated all objects on which he could perform the same action of sitting down as chairs, and sprang up. In fact, on the command "chair" he treated a variety of other objects such as boxes, podia and overturned stools as chairs; which was an action appropriate to a dog but not to a man, for many of these objects were definitely not suitable for people to sit on.'⁹

Has this got anything to say about environmental problems? They are certainly problems of perception, taking perception once more in its wider sense, and result from actions which are wrong or simply inadequate. Are they also problems of perception in the sense that they are based on wrong or inadequate thought and observation? This was certainly true in the case of the man in Naples. Not only did he not know how to deal with the landscape and art there, but he did not even see or feel it. His visual impressions brought him no joy, no understanding and no experience. Are we like him in our failure to notice the extinction of species?

The symptoms are similar. Uexküll found fault with the
public as early as 1907, complaining that people strolling in the
country saw nothing, and were content simply to recognize
familiar objects, and even these only in a restricted fashion.
'The world which they see when out walking is made up of only
three or four things – paths, trees, houses and dogs. That is
all.'[10] It is striking in connection with this list that the dying
forests have had a great effect on the public, an effect almost
irreconcilable with the fact that the statistical data relating to
the extinction of other species have in general hardly been
noticed, or at least have been registered without visible reaction. Could this perhaps have something to do with the special
relationship of the German soul to the German forest?

I have a better explanation, which will take us further.
With the death of the forests the extinction of species has
reached Uexküll's minimal list, of paths, trees, houses and
dogs. In the case of trees we can actually see the way in which
our environment is dying. Otherwise, we do not notice extinction: at most, we read about it. The gentian, the corn-cockle, the
diamond fern, the orchid, the fly-trap, the wild rose and many
others are all disappearing slowly, if not already extinct. If we
had noticed this as it was actually happening, we should
probably have become alarmed much earlier – long before the
forests began to die.

*We are only really affected by the destruction of the
connatural world when this destruction is marching on faster
than the simultaneous degeneration of our senses.* Maybe environmental ruin has only progressed so far because our senses
too have died or degenerated; not in a physiological sense, but
because we have nothing more to do with the world around us,
so that the impressions of our senses can no longer reach our
hearts. This means, of course, that the cultivation of the senses
is one of the most important requirements of a new environmental politics. There is a huge task here for today's society,
and particularly for artists. Even in schools the education of the
senses is almost criminally neglected, in favour of the development of cognitive understanding.

This seems to explain how we have got to where we stand

now. Cognitive information has never moved humanity except when brought alive by the senses. Does it follow from this that we will only take serious notice of the foreseeable change in climate when we can feel it? Public awareness of this issue has really only arisen because the future which will derive from the current warming, with droughts and an increased number of storms, seems already to have begun. So is it inevitable that insights about long-term developments will only occur when it is already too late to prevent the changes? This does not have to be the case. Any concern is rooted in the feelings which lead our knowledge and actions, and these are touched by the perception of the senses as well. I believe that we should be able to visualize the consequences of our actions if these can be predicted, and so be affected by them even if they cannot be felt sensorily at that particular time. My hypothesis is valid if feelings are included within the concept of senses, as they were in the Greek *aisthesis*. This is the concept I adhere to in what follows.

The idea that you can only appeal to rational self-interest is one of the most irrational in environmental politics. A political will is first formed when something moves people, not primarily because of their interests, but within their hearts. Admittedly this motivation may also include such interests, whether personal or general, when the heart is home to them. Such perception from the heart is essential. It can link a new awareness with a new consciousness and a new way of acting, based on the revival of the senses. It will come into being when we do not merely read about, but feel for ourselves, what it is we are doing, and realize that it really is *we* who are doing it. Environmental politics, which are the concern not just of our world but of the worlds of every species, have no chance of success as long as this change is either vetoed or suppressed.

To take an example: our perception of the car does not normally come sufficiently from the heart. Imagine a car which is sleek, fast and comfortable. The doors close with a satisfying sound, the engine throbs with restrained power. This vehicle would be so like the ideal of the legendary pioneers of car manufacturing that they would cheer to see it surge past. Let

us analyse what there is to cheer about. Though I can still
understand what sounded like progress and freedom, what I
hear above everything in the roar of the engine is the violence
done to our natural environment – human beings, animals,
plants and the atmosphere – three thousand poisonous shots a
minute with this reading on the rev counter. Should we really
not be ashamed that we expect people and other living beings
to breathe in these petrol fumes, quite apart from the way we
are contributing to a future climatic catastrophe, and also
endangering the lives of others? Every third person killed in
road accidents is indeed a 'third party': a pedestrian or a cyclist.
What is there to cheer about, when we have grasped these facts
of car travel? Why do we do it? More than half the mileage of
individual motor traffic is for pleasure or holidays. Cars look
and sound different when we become aware of all this.

Revival of the senses should also lead to some less dramatic changes in behaviour. For instance, we might stop having
electric lights on during the day. This is not just a matter of
saving energy, but at least as much a question of attitude;
whether one is thankful for the light of the sun as long as it
shines, or behaves as if in view of our technical abilities we have
no expectations from it any longer. As a member of a number of
enquiry commissions in the German parliament it always
annoyed me greatly that even in bright daylight we would sit
behind closed curtains (net curtains as high up as the twenty-
ninth floor), and that artificial light (sixty lights, admittedly
energy saving lamps, in a room with an area of 140m^2 and
north-facing windows covering an area of 60m^2) was always
required. I was allowed to open the curtains, but whenever I
surreptitiously turned off the lights, for instance during the
lunch break, someone would always say, 'Can we have some
light, please? – I can't see a thing.' Artificial light was what was
meant: in sunlight they could no longer see. Does this symbolic
darkness not characterize all political processes concerned with
the perception of nature?

Everyone, however placed, can begin to cultivate the
senses, so that the smokescreen which hides from us the cost of
living in today's industrial society is dispersed. For guidance we

can turn to Hugo Kükelhaus, one of the first to think of educating the senses.[11]

The two examples already given have shown that the preservation of our senses affects not only the senses, but also our whole scheme of perceptual reference, and so our whole life. Either we hear an engine differently, and travel more often on foot or by bicycle, and less frequently by car and with a different outlook, or we simply have not changed our perception of the sound of an engine. Sunlight and artificial light must similarly be treated differently, or nothing has changed.

The keyword is action. The environment of the hard-working self-made man we talked about earlier had degenerated to such an extent during his one-sided working life that even Naples held no excitement for him. It is not enough to be informed about species extinction or recognize other areas of destruction when an expert shows us the last few individuals of a species which is dying out. We must also *do* something once again with what has been forgotten, suppressed and isolated. Environmental problems are problems of perception in the full sense, requiring not only observation, but also attentive action, whether it is to do with cars, light, or anything else.

The environment degenerates and disintegrates where perception, which knits together awareness and action, is no longer cultivated. We need to become active in areas we have forsaken, to re-engage with animals, plants, landscape and the elements. As long as the species which die out in our own continent are those we have nothing to do with, we are not disturbed in the least. There is no private or political reason to get involved in putting an end to environmental destruction, as long as we remain satisfied that somewhere it is still possible to take a walk in green surroundings, whether in a spruce plantation or among eight different types of easy-care, pollution-resistant cotoneaster from the municipal gardening service.

How do we reach a point where we are no longer satisfied by sterility? The best way is to experience the creative joy of bringing more life into the world. Maybe one day somebody meets an old friend, among the many others completely satis-

fied by ready-made greenery. This friend says, 'Do you know
what I was doing last weekend? In our district there was once
a brook meandering through between the gardens. I've seen old
photos of it, with everything looking very much alive. But there
were floods from time to time, so the authorities put it into a
channel to improve drainage. Then we heard of the action taken
by a group somewhere a similar thing had happened. They
freed the brook from the bed it had been forced into, so that it
doesn't just flow past, but lingers a bit and creates a whole new
environment for animals and plants. Now we're doing this too,
and you simply wouldn't believe how much fun it is to do
something just to enjoy water flowing, or for animals and
plants, and not for commercial reasons or anything like that. I
feel I'm becoming that much freer when I'm freeing the stream
from its concrete bed. In the end it isn't just the streams which
have been encased in concrete...'

Hearing this tale, the other man may think 'He's crazy.
Incurable romantics, these greenies. After all, the only reason
for a stream's existence is to carry away rain water. My children
come home from school with the same sort of stories, about how
they've created an "eco-pond" or something. It's very fashion-
able at the moment, but it'll soon be over! My experiences of
freedom always come most easily when I'm at the wheel of my
car...'

But something of such encounters usually sticks, particularly with those who fight against this kind of project most
fiercely, and try to play the role of rationality in person (by this
I mean the kind of rationality which sees brooks not as water
courses, but simply as channels and if need be drains for
sewage). This man – it seems that men succumb to this kind of
rationale more easily than women – may well think about the
situation at some stage, if stories like this one about the freeing
of a stream are told to him more often, and his children keep
telling him about things they have done at school. Perhaps he
might be stuck in a traffic jam in his car, and have time to
ponder 'Why in fact am I here doing this? When I first had a car
many years ago I was one of about two hundred thousand
people in the country, and at that stage driving was still

enjoyable, and gave a real sense of freedom, or at least of independence. My wife says we shouldn't confuse the two – we should tell the motoring organizations that sometime. But what's come of it? Now I'm stuck in a mess of metal and waste gases, surrounded by tarmac, sitting in a comfortably upholstered hole, catching just the odd glimpse of a living thing in the distance, that is apart from the other drivers, who all look pretty glazed in any case. Is it really worthwhile to spend, all in all, a sixth of my salary, or in other words to work a good hour every day, for this kind of independence?'

Agriculture is one area where people experience contact with the connatural world, and where the senses could be cultivated. Nowadays, though, two or three workers are enough to support a hundred people, and because operations are on an industrial scale there is no longer culture in agriculture; these two or three no longer really have anything to do with the animals and plants in their care. Since even a more sensible and ecologically justifiable system of agriculture would probably require only five or six workers to support a hundred people, in general we must regain this experiential perception of the natural world through other forms of activity.

Even in a hectic lifestyle, this could happen through dealing with plants, as gardeners do. Here contact with earth and water is combined with experience of air and light. Being out in the open air gives one a chance to escape from the constrictions of a flat, and at the same time to experience another life in itself. To wait in stillness and watch how something comes into being of its own accord is a calming exercise, particularly for people who otherwise tend to think that without them nothing would be achieved.

Any kind of travel also works against the decline of the senses, as long as it is not merely overcoming distance, but a genuine experiencing of the route: for example walking or hiking, cycling and sailing. Heraclitus' dictum 'The way up and down – one and the same' can only be properly understood when the paradox within it is recognized. Are the hard ascent of a mountain, until one finally reaches the top, and the much easier descent, not as different from one another as hot and cold, or wet and dry? And yet, astonishingly, it is the same way in each direction. The walker and the cyclist experience this. The car driver, by contrast, simply says, 'Of course it's the same way in each direction, I feel no difference at all.' In fact in a car one simply doesn't notice. Much eludes the car driver. For example, he gains his picture of a town only from the traffic lanes.

From a bicycle one can experience what lies beyond these lanes, and see the quiet residential streets and the unglazed people talking to each other. In addition one has the immediacy of light and air, damp and sunshine. Saying that cyclists are always getting soaked is an excuse used by drivers to cover themselves. It actually rains relatively infrequently, even in notoriously wet places like Hamburg, and when it does one can easily take shelter. One rarely gets a cold, never has a parking problem, and for most town journeys of from three to five miles a bicycle is even quicker than a car.

The third mode of travel I mentioned is sailing. We mostly experience the four elements only as they are required by plants for growth. But earth, water, air and fire are not merely the essentials of plant life: each has its own qualities. In sailing, these are experienced for what they are. The boat is a piece of earth which carries me, but in its movement I feel the water, the gentle strength of the carrying force which surrounds me. The water is moved by the wind, forming the waves which extend to the horizon, as water and air affect each other. The boat moves too, as the wind strikes the sail. And where does the wind come from? Its strength is that of the sun, of fire, which moves the atmosphere through warmth. I see the waves and the clouds, hear the roar of the water and also the movement of the rigging in the wind, smell the wind and the water, while sensing movement and within it the combination of elements.

Working against the degeneration of the senses by return-ing to forgotten realms of life also requires teaching and information, environmental education in the widest sense. This is generally held to mean that a new consciousness must be created, beginning with children, and so requiring at least a generation before it becomes widespread. I believe this view to be false. The environmental and energy movements of the seventies and eighties showed that even in the timespan of half a generation there can be an astonishing change in public awareness. In any case, change cannot begin with children, because they are educated by adults. The new consciousness must have its roots in these adults, so that they can pass it on to the children.

But where can schoolchildren obtain the education, necessary to preserve the basis for life and revive the senses, when many biology teachers can no longer distinguish a winter lime from a summer one? And while in the higher classes they prefer to teach the biochemistry which is taught in the first semester of university courses? And how should the biology teachers have such knowledge, when their own teachers, the professors, nowadays hardly understand anything of natural history either? When the professors themselves do have a knowledge of plants and animals they sometimes make up for what was neglected at school by teaching elementary botany in the first semester of a university course, but would it not be preferable to reverse the process by studying natural history in school? Even better, in this way more teachers and professors might themselves take part in the environmental movement, and contribute their own ideas to it, strengthening support for environmentally responsible courses of action. In order to revivify the natural world in our awareness and our actions, it is absolutely essential that human activity should respect the individuality of other species' environments. To do this properly, we shall have to start new activities, such as reviving lost 'spheres of functioning'; and we shall also have to give up much of what we have been doing up to now.

Breaking Away from the Consumer Society

Any change in consumer behaviour must combine acting in new ways with rejecting the old. This is critical for two reasons. The first is that in an industrial country such as Germany, more than half the gross national product is spent on private consumption, while a fifth is invested (this figure includes house-

hold investments, such as houses, cars, etc.), and a further fifth
is spent by the state. If we take the national product not as a
measure of economic success, but as a measure of the destruction linked to it, then individual consumers have a two thirds
share in it. The interests of industry are by no means solely
responsible. They should not be underestimated, but why do
they succeed? For instance, the power of the motor industry,
though it is a very real power, rests on the fact that about two
thirds of the population travel regularly by car.

The second reason is that many people feel themselves
exposed to hazards at the mercy of the industrial economy,
unable to do anything against it. As a result some develop a
helpless anger against the circumstances within society which
permit such hazards. Others find this powerlessness quite
comfortable, in that they are able to live with a better conscience than they otherwise could, having pushed the responsibility onto others. To the first group, I say that they have
resigned themselves too quickly, to the second, that they are
making life too easy for themselves. If we all work together we
are undoubtedly capable of changing things.

To take driving as an example: an astonishingly large
number of people have entirely stopped travelling by car. I have
a beneficial suggestion for those who are unwilling or unable to
go that far: each year every fifth person should cut out every
fifth journey. Is this too high a goal? One could certainly begin
with the journeys to the letter box and the hairdresser. A tenth
of all local and regional car journeys (up to 30 miles) are less
than half a mile, half less than three, and two thirds less than
six.[12] Anyone who occasionally does without the car on such
journeys, and goes on foot or by bike, soon notices that these
modes of transport have their own attractions, and are not a
sacrifice.

Car ownership cannot become universal, but only a gradual
move away from it can solve more problems than it creates at
first. All the same, the modest restraint I have suggested would
reduce the number of journeys made each year by 4%, and
would in ten years reduce traffic by one third. Political action I
hold to be equally important. Once such a movement had

started, it would be possible to follow the Scandinavian example of allowing into towns only cars with drivers who have
tickets for public transport, so that the public transport system
could be improved and towns increasingly closed to cars. Such
a mass move away from cars would leave the motor industry
sufficient time to divert its undoubted intelligence towards
more advanced and less destructive products.

Meat consumption is another area for action. In Germany
in 1988 it stood at 6.4 million tonnes of live weight per annum,
or 104 kg per person. A third of this is wasted or used as animal
food, while two thirds is eaten by people: half a pound per day
on average, babies and vegetarians included. Meat is relatively
cheap – but the costs are cruelty to animals, factory farming and
the import of cheap fodder from the Third World. It would be
healthier to eat at most half as much meat, and if the price was
then doubled, so that the total spent on it was no more than
before, the animals could be kept in such a way that they would
at least have had a life worth living before they were slaughtered. A price increase of between two and three pence per egg
would be enough to achieve this in the case of laying hens. If this
means that some people are too poor to buy enough eggs, then
instead of supporting cruelty to animals we should be doing
something about poverty.

Groceries have been getting steadily cheaper for many
years, and the connatural world is paying the price. And what
do we do with the money we save? To take the example of
Germany, we learn from the 1989 *Statistical Year Book* that in
1988 a four person household with average income (2,900-4,400
DM per month) spent an average 516 DM per month on food
(excluding drinks, tobacco and meals out, otherwise the figure
would be 767 DM). This can only happen because of cheap
provisions. The average expenditure on rent and energy is 854
DM. And how much does the same household spend on the car?
The year book tells us this too – 488 DM per month, including
of course the costs of purchase.

So about 15% of income is spent on food, where savings are
made, and these savings are spent on the car, which costs
almost as much. One salary group higher (income 5,200-7,000

DM per month) cars cost more than food. The monthly average amounts to 630 DM on food and 638 DM on the car, or cars. Moreover, these two amounts can be brought into a direct connection with one another, for the proportion of income spent on food, in the continuous prosperity of the last twenty-five years, has been approximately halved: we can see what has been done with the other half. The savings made, through an industrial agriculture based on cruelty to animals and destruction of the landscape, have been spent on the car. Two of the worst existing sources of environmental destruction, for which the private consumer is directly responsible, facilitate and reinforce each other. As long as this is the case, consumers, whether individually or together, can withdraw from this cartel of destruction by buying other products. If your feeling of powerlessness makes you suffer, you can take heart from this; but anyone who likes being powerless and puts forward various reasons why nothing can be done against capitalism, or at least certainly not by individuals, should realize that this comfortable feeling is a fallacy.

New consumer behaviour should move towards a situation where products are no longer sold more cheaply than they are in reality, at the expense of the connatural world, of future generations, and of the Third World. Obviously this aim cannot be achieved at once, particularly in view of the supply of goods which exists at present. We must simply begin in the most effective way we can. No one individual can discover all the things which damage the environment through their production, in consumption, or as waste products. To do this would mean being occupied round the clock. But considerable pressure could be exerted on the economy from grass roots level if more action groups were formed. Using self-help and the literature which is either available or emerging they could look into some questions such as:

– Where does the meat in our shops come from?

– Which household cleaning agents are still justifiable?

– Where can we obtain natural and uncontaminated vegetables at a reasonable price?

— How can we make energy savings at home and in public buildings?

— What can be done to avoid waste or recycle it, beginning with buying suitable products? etc.

The direct marketing of foodstuffs by farmers conscious of the environment can offer good co-operative opportunities through such initiatives. This can help stabilize small farms. By buying foodstuffs at prices which are not below their worth, everyone can contribute to the preservation of at least the last vestiges of culture in agri-culture. The cheap products of the huge agro-industrial companies will cost us dear in the end. Many small shops are gradually going over to catering for the ecologically minded customer. The freedom to consume means not only independence but responsibility in buying things. Awareness and action must be consistent even in consumer behaviour. Consumer trends are what a market economy responds to most readily, and this is one of its greatest virtues.

The responsibility of consumers is different from what it used to be, not only in buying particular products, but also because of the global implications of most buying decisions. The building of an environmentally friendly house begins with the choice of an appropriate site, allowing for as many south-facing windows as possible and a winter garden at the back, using suitable building materials etc. But this is by no means enough. The very best architecture is far from achieving an environmentally friendly house, if the site can only be reached by car. We have been in the habit of using cars to get round problems, but in a global future this can no longer be justified. Towns must fit the countryside which supports them, and this should be true even when that 'countryside' is as far away as Brazil, if meat is bought which has been reared on fodder grown there. Another important aspect of an environmentally friendly house is of course that energy consumption should not contribute to climate change. Normally one does not need hot water to wash one's hands, and people who heat their houses so much in winter that they can wear summer clothing inside should consider the price to be paid. We should not think of ourselves as living only in our own homes: each of us lives not only in a house, but also in a town, in a country, on a continent and on the earth as a whole.

Will consumers with such a global outlook ever exist? Neo-classical economic theory assumes that a person wants first to have more and more possessions, and secondly to have more than other people. This *Homo economicus*, led from without, has no defence against the battery of goods for sale, and is not the autonomous consumer who wishes to live his life among other people, and who knows how to say no both politically and economically when he doesn't want something. According to surveys by Scherhorn[13] the 'autonomously oriented' – people who combine increasing affluence with independent outlook – do not buy more and more goods as their first requirement; their buying decisions are directed rather by the use they intend to make of their purchases. The more self-assured one is, the less need to base a sense of self-esteem on having more than other people. In the light of these surveys, a chance for preserving the requirements for life lies in responsible citizens becoming the right sort of consumers.

The influence of a change in consumer behaviour can be even stronger politically than economically, since, while the general public has only a two thirds control over the economy, it should, at least at election time, have a one hundred per cent control over the political scene. Voters who wake in their consumer behaviour from their comfortable dream of power-lessness will support those who will no longer permit us – consumers and producers, employers and employees – to live at the cost of damage to the connatural world, to posterity and to the Third World. Political parties would do well to support this aim, since they have a constitutional obligation to contribute to the development of political opinion, even if they are far from having sole responsibility. They need to be shown that respon-sible citizens can take action outside political parties. Of course, it is also true, that problems cannot all be solved by the actions of individuals. By beginning at home one strengthens political will at the base with one's own credibility, but this will must then be organized and carried into the political system.

What I recommend is a peaceful consumer revolution. We require ecological disobedience, if we are to accomplish more than the government thinks fit. The revolution is necessary because the life-threatening course of our economy is the greatest problem facing us, and because the best way of coming to grips with the economy is by removing economic acceptance. There is then room for political change, whereas political actions can scarcely have any effect on the economy if everything produced continues to be bought. If nothing changes, then the conundrum of the environmental crisis cannot be solved. To see the causes only in big business is an illusion. We must not forget that in reality it is the consumers – all of us – who sanction the economic situation by our purchases, and it is also through us that the economy is able to assert itself politically.

It is important to realize that this life-destroying economy is *our* economy, and that the very same people who voice complaints about environmental destruction often promote it by their actions. Opinion polls about priorities in protecting the environment show that the worries creeping up on us are often expressed, but such consternation is often not enough to cause a change in behaviour.

The economy is not just big business: it is all of us. We take part in it not only as consumers, but also as employees, in wage negotiations, for instance. These should not be simply about income and working hours, but also about better and fairer working conditions and management relations. But in this time of environmental crisis, surely humanization of the workplace should be accompanied by a humanization of business itself, in its dealings with the connatural world. Many jobs can only be sustained at the cost of the environment. They are under threat when a company is no longer allowed to pollute the air, the water or the earth. Is it not doubly inhuman, both to workers and to the connatural world, when people have to earn their living at the expense of the environment? How can we permit a situation where our rich society expects people to earn their living from work which produces more damage than benefits?

Our economy offers a sorry picture when we take a look at companies which would like to combine their business interests with greater responsibility towards the environment. Their spokesmen say that as long as it is not forbidden to make profits from despoiling the environment, they must carry on doing so: otherwise their competitors would continue anyway, and gain a commercial advantage. Can it really be the intention of a free economy that abuses should only be avoided or stopped when they become forbidden?

Take as an example the ozone layer in the stratosphere, which is destroyed by chlorofluorocarbons (CFCs), something that has been acknowledged for several years now. When this became known, the companies which manufacture and process these substances should, out of decency, have declared, 'We are horrified to learn that by our actions over many years we have been endangering humanity and the connatural world to an ever greater extent. We want to put a stop to this as soon as possible, and to repair as far as we can the damage we caused when we were still unaware of what we were doing. However, this task will be too much for us as individual companies. So we are asking for public support, particularly for appropriate legislation, so that we can recycle the CFCs from scrapped refrigerators for example.'

Sadly, though, not one of the affected companies said anything of the sort. Far from it: I even heard, during a hearing of the German climate commission in May 1988, that in certain sectors CFCs were 'vital' to industrial society. The example given was that of a plastics foam for refrigerator insulation, since this was the only way to manage with walls three centimetres thick, while otherwise it could not be done with less than six centimetres. Do these gentlemen simply not think about what is *actually* vital – protecting the very basis of life, especially in the Southern Hemisphere, from the effects of ultraviolet radiation? Should companies which think and behave in such an irresponsible way be allowed, at the same time, to take advantage of their constitutionally guaranteed freedom? In the meantime, another company within the field declared that a substitute had been found which would allow the walls to remain at a width of three centimetres. The response of a third company was that during the transitional period the use of the old substances would have to continue, otherwise jobs would be put at risk. This kind of short-sightedness would be simply pitiful, if the dangers were not so great; but to react to them in such a restricted way is as blinkered as it is irresponsible. In spite of all this, as far as I can see the production and use of CFCs in Germany will cease in line with the climate commission's recommendations. If this does happen, the success will be largely due to a change in consumer consciousness, which has prompted many companies to advertise that materials containing CFCs no longer form part of their products. But why must such advances always have to be fought for *against* the economy?

I am sorry to say that this was not just a case of narrow-minded reactions from those affected. A respected daily newspaper gave an equally restricted and one-sided assessment in its economic section: 'Profits will suffer as a result of CFC discussions',[14] and did not mention who and what suffered as a result of CFC use. Shortly afterwards the same newspaper ran an article entitled 'The years of ethics are numbered', to the satisfaction of one industrialist who was tired of continually being invited to lecture about the responsibilities of industry to society. He claimed that the German economy should finally stop 'wanting to be good', (something it has in my opinion never even begun) and 'should again become what it is in reality – business-minded'. Business is not about ethics, but about turnover and profit.[15]

I wish such opinions were not representative. But I would be very interested to know of businesses which behave in a way so fundamentally different from this as to alter the total picture appreciably. We need the economy, to solve with its help problems which without it would never have existed. I have no doubt that it will react flexibly to a consumer revolution, by looking to its profits; but are there no longer any responsible factions who might join the revolution themselves?

In general, the unions present just as bad a picture. Do they ever think of anything but themselves? One would certainly not automatically credit the mining and chemical unions with a wider horizon than their employers. The efforts of our metalworkers' union are more hopeful: it has spoken out not only for workers' interests, but is looking for participation in decisions about the kind and quality of the manufactured products as well. However good the pay and conditions, they should not be the sole aim of union politics, if the products are atomic, biological or chemical weapons. Is this not also true for CFCs, herbicides, and for many things which are sold by exploiting human weakness, even cars perhaps, or at least those without catalytic convertors?

Could employers and employees not accommodate the voice of nature for once in their wage negotiations? For example the German railway has finally discovered how the Swiss system of half-price passes can usefully be transferred to our situation. Every ticket is half-price on possession of this pass, which is valid for one year. Travelling by train then becomes even cheaper than the petrol for the corresponding car journey. This is decisive in practical comparison, because otherwise the average costs of the railway compete against the marginal costs of car driving. The unions could negotiate for workers to benefit from an employers' contribution of a half-price pass. Swiss teachers are already so far along this road that the rail pass forms part of their salary.

We have direct control over almost two thirds of all funds spent on a day-to-day basis, year after year. If we would in future ask ourselves every time we think about buying anything, to what extent the purchase will increase the burden on the connatural world, posterity or the Third World, would that not be a wonderful revolution? A revolution it would certainly be, a turnround in the criteria by which we keep house, but above all a turnround in general awareness and so in our circumstances, a *wonderful* revolution. The ruling consciousness must change, then our political rulers will change too, quite easily in a democracy.

In contrast to the butchery of the French and Russian revolutions, the East German uprising has shown how prevailing circumstances can be overcome by non-violent resistance. But the resulting reunion of East and West Germany has simply produced a self-satisfaction in our country, which threatens to deflect attention from our own unsolved and pressing problems. It would have been right to use the East German revolution as a cue for the completely different revolution needed at home, which seems difficult only because it could be so easy: the revolution against a life-threatening economy and our own inertia, against living in what passes for prosperity at the expense of the connatural world, of posterity and of the Third World. I am sure that our capitalist economy could survive such a revolution, and could produce goods which consumers who think for themselves would wish to purchase. The real problem is whether we, the general public, really want this change. The remaining chapters of this book consider what such a change would require, and the implications for the state and for society.

Notes

[1] *Laws* 777d
[2] *Werke* vol.13, 324
[3] Uexküll 1940/1956, 47
[4] Uexküll 1934/1956, 28
[5] ibid. 29
[6] Uexküll 1909/1921, 45
[7] Uexküll 1907, 660ff
[8] Uexküll 1934/1956, 68
[9] ibid., 67
[10] Uexküll 1907, 659f
[11] Kükelhaus 1973; 1982
[12] Kloas/Kuhfeld 1987
[13] Scherhorn 1988
[14] *Frankfurter Allgemeine Zeitung*, 31-3-90
[15] *Frankfurter Allgemeine Zeitung*, 17-4-90

Chapter 2

From Human Environment to Connatural World

For ecological reasons, we can no longer think of the world simply as the human environment. The cosmos is not just humanity's living space. This must be realized in industrial society's patterns of action. Since these, however, are knit together with our patterns of thought and awareness, a change in behaviour will only happen when we recognize that destructive activity stems from a complementary mode of thought. Cultivation of the senses can provide an opportunity for such recognition. Provided sense-derived feeling for the natural environment does not fade away more quickly than ruin advances, direct experience of the consequences of the industrial economic process may create the outrage necessary for promoting a political will to restrict that process.

Everyone can contribute to the non-violent revolution of autonomous consumers, and everyone can persuade others to do the same. Say to begin with one person in a thousand withdraws support from our destructive economy, and in the course of a year convinces one other person to do the same: that would be 0.2% of the population in only one year. If this twofold increase were repeated in the following year after two years the figure would be 0.4%, after three 0.8%, after five 3.2% and after eight 25.6%. After barely ten years the figure would be 100%. By that time, if not before, even the government would be included.

Instead of growth in destruction we need growth in resistance against it. If there is no change in behaviour, and the basis of life continues to be eroded, it will not be because the general public *cannot* do anything against the destructive force of the economy, but because it *will* not. People who say that the work of destruction must be halted, then carry on blithely as before, cannot really be convinced that they are following the wrong path. But of course by declaring support in principle for environmental protection, they have the comfort of voicing their objections, and perhaps even the doubts they usually keep concealed. Besides, they can complain that they live under circumstances which individuals are powerless to alter.

During the transition period, when the alarm raised by the senses has not been answered by a change in lifestyle, it is understandable that people should fundamentally approve of protecting the environment without making the connection between destructive behaviour and the way of thought which fosters it. A responsible consumer society can only be formed slowly, particularly when the economy and advertising offer every incentive for people to abrogate any authentic economic will, and to submit instead to outside influences. A general consensus may indicate a readiness to change the relationship of the industrial economy with nature, even if this does not lead immediately to a change in behaviour. So if life is to be enriched, it is essential to save the senses from atrophy, and to be less obsessed with the acquisition of goods.

Anyone so alarmed by the message of the senses as to break away from the old pattern of thought and the destructive behaviour linked to it must certainly look ahead to a new way of thinking. A reviving sensory contact with the natural world should then reveal, not only that the present economy is irresponsible within nature, but why it is so, and how such responsibility should be addressed in the future. Without this gut-feeling to start with, the most rational arguments can usually achieve nothing at all. But our industrial society, centred on an economy organized around science and technology, promulgates a mental picture of the world so closed that it should be rejected by reasons beyond emotional and sensory grounds. We must identify and account for what has been done wrong, and for what should be done instead. This and the following chapter deal with these reasons.

Justifying a whole process is as a rule more difficult than justifying the next step. This is especially true of new approaches. For instance, where criticism has been levelled against my ideas for achieving peace with nature, it has usually arisen because I no longer share assumptions which are so commonplace that their linkage with destructive behaviour is simply not noticed. Deviant opinions are thrust aside, due to the impossible desire to adjust reason to conformity when one's own position looks like being called into question. For example, someone who believes that the rest of the world is there simply for our use may feel that this is reasonable in itself, while there is a substantial need to prove the opposing assumption that the natural world of itself has intrinsic value.

In my view, the orthodox recommendation for a way forward without any fundamental change in direction is merely a continued approach to the abyss, though with rather better footwear than before. Instead of accepting the current arguments, let us look at what can be learned from the past, by examining the present situation from a historical perspective. As I hope to show, the present rationality of our behaviour is revealed as an unfinished enlightenment.

Some historians say that the only thing we can learn from history is that there is nothing to learn from it. Yet in history we learn how past conceptual developments can be taken up and adapted to the future. Insofar as today's points of reference lie in the present, their historical nature does not occur to us. Starting from the discovery that our world is not the whole world, and that other species live in environments other than our own, but all with their own value within the natural order, I shall choose as my historical link the progressive insight that all people are part of the human community, of humanity.

From Enlightenment about Humanity to Enlightenment about Nature

In our value system and in our laws, it is undisputed that damage should never be inflicted upon general well-being. What is meant by 'general' well-being, though? For the purposes of assessing damage to the common good, the whole can be viewed either as humanity and *its* natural environment, or as humanity and *the* connatural world. In terms of political philosophy, constitutional law and industrial activity this is a wide-reaching difference. In the first case we would have to take the future into account, so that a resource from which we live should not be unintelligently squandered. Environmental destruction would only be forbidden if people were affected by it, including future generations This corresponds to the aim of and justification for environmental politics up to now. In the second case we would have a wider responsibility, shielding the environment from our activities not only where a present or future harm to humanity was likely to result, but also taking into account the intrinsic value of the connatural world within nature's whole. This is the way I recommend to achieve peace with nature. Till now, this idea has gained only minority support.

I shall make the difference clearer by reference to the basic social question of the nineteenth century, the exploitation of human beings by their fellows in the early capitalist economy. That the exploited should also be taken into account in any assessment of the common interest could be argued along two lines. On the one hand it was thought prudent to preserve as far as possible the labouring capacity of the workers, in order to maximize profit. Really poor wages would mean a corresponding decrease in profits, as well as necessitating a disproportionate number of police to provide protection against theft and unrest. From the commercial standpoint it was completely unprofitable to pay wages which left the workers hungry. The conclusion would have been that workers' conditions should be improved as far as this was to the advantage of the proprietors. The other argument ran as follows: 'Those we are treating as slaves are human beings like ourselves. We are responsible for them, and the way we are treating them offends against human dignity, theirs as well as ours. They belong to the same common humanity as we do, so the common interest is something we share.' It is difficult to say for sure which of these two lines of reasoning was decisive at particular stages in history. The actual result corresponds more closely to the second, and today there is scarcely anyone who would want to justify social justice or a social state solely on grounds of self-interest.

At the end of the nineteenth century it was beyond dispute that general well-being referred not only to capitalists, but also to the workers subject to the new economic system and to the lower-middle classes. Having arrived at a position of enlightenment on the common humanity of all human beings, it was difficult for anyone to go back on this consciousness, by maintaining that some people should have less stake in the general interest than others. The conclusion that all people enter the world as equals, and that this equality must be preserved in the political community, was unchallenged even at that time, and lies at the constitutional heart of the modern state.

So far, the role of humanity within nature has not been subject to a similar enlightenment. My plea is that this first enlightenment concerning human equality within nature, our being born equal, should be extended further to cover our natural relationship with the rest of the world. Both enlightenments have far-reaching, if divergent, political consequences.

Humanity's Common Birthright

Such a second enlightenment, or fulfilment of the first, taking nature into account, may well come as a surprise to some people. It may seem self-evident that all human beings are equal fellow creatures, while this equality – being human – does not exist between humanity and the connatural world. I would first like to remind anyone who thinks this way that the recognition of all human beings as equals is not as self-evident as it usually appears to educated people in the developed industrial nations of the world, who themselves constitute only a small percentage of the world's population.

The recognition of a common humanity comes relatively easily to an enlightened perception such as ours – particularly since our ancestors murdered most of those people whom they did not recognize as humans, but held to be savages. Recalling the former inhabitants of different parts of the globe, who were wiped out by the white man, one can give only faint praise to the enlightened fellowship of the conquerors' descendants. Furthermore, a comparison of the former colonization of foreign peoples with today's colonization of the connatural world shows us not only that the conquerors unrestrainedly murdered these 'savages' not yet regarded as fellows, but also that such action was again linked to a corresponding rationale which legitimized it.

That human beings living under comparatively primitive conditions appear savage and almost animal-like to civilized peoples is a truism that has been handed down from ancient times, for example in the description of the Ethiopians by the Roman historian Diodorus Siculus (1st century BC) in the third book of his *Bibliotheca Historica*. But such observations do not have to ignore the overlaps between the world of humans and that of animals, and should recognize that the differences are only of degree. Yet the conquerors who had an interest in robbing foreign peoples whilst keeping as clear a conscience about it as possible found here an irreconcilable antithesis. A prime example is the Spaniard Fernández de Oviedo (1478-1557), who was regarded in his time as an expert in Indian matters; he travelled a great deal, and, as one of Charles V's chroniclers, wrote a general and natural history of the West Indies in more than a dozen volumes. In an essay which is well worth reading[1] Mario Erdheim has presented his thought in the context of his time.

This is how Oviedo described the Indians: 'In the same way as they have thick skulls their mentality is animal-like, and equally averse to rationality.'[2] What was, in his opinion, especially animal-like was their irrepressible sexuality. For example a chief of whom he gives a report was supposed to have had thirty wives, 'but not only for his use in such union as is usual between married men and their wives, but in order to commit other bestial and shameful sins'.[3] The Indians were, above all, committed to excessive sensuality of the first degree. 'Their principle aspirations were to eat, to drink, and to feast, to satisfy their lust and serve their idols, and to abandon themselves to many other filthy and bestial vices.'[4]

There were even theological disputes about whether the Indians were human beings or animals, and this doubt reflected the state of Spanish interests. What Oviedo the expert reported to his king about the Indians was fairly erroneous with respect to them, but it nonetheless gave a completely accurate description of a 'world of perception', in Uexküll's term, fitting knowledge to the interests of the ruling Spanish crown. The objectivity and expertise of his description lay in this very unity. It corresponds to classical science, which also, although at a perceptibly higher level, constructs a similar tidy picture of the world, which is to be made use of in a very definite way.

Whether or not classical science – and of course quantum theory gives a different picture – says more about industrial society than about nature is a question I would prefer to leave for the moment. It is clear, however, that Oviedo's portrayal of foreign peoples says more about the situation in Spain than about the situation in the West Indies. 'Attitudes towards foreign culture are always a mirror of attitudes towards suppressed areas of one's own culture'. Instead of criticizing the drop in moral standards among the Spanish nobility, Oviedo devoted himself to writing what is actually an anachronistic romance of chivalry, while describing the 'filthiness' of the Indians as 'bestial'.

This way of thinking was bound up with colonial interests. But how far have we managed to overcome it today? Well into the last century Indians were still being murdered as 'savages' in North America, while slaves were designated 'chattels' in law. Even at the present time equal status has not been universally granted to all coloured people. Among the descendants of the victors and of the races they decimated, the equality of all humanity is still far from being recognized. As a rule other races are no longer described as bestial, but why does racial discrimination still exist in many countries, not just in South Africa, if not because many people continue to think that other human beings are not as human as they are, and should be treated accordingly? Nor does this happen only abroad; it was we Germans who, in the recent past, allowed the murder of the Jews on account of their race. All too often we fail to accept foreigners living in our country without reservation as fellow human beings. And finally in our society a woman nearly always has to achieve more than a man, in order to be regarded as equally well-qualified.

The equality of all people is certainly not as self-evident as those who pay it lip-service like to think; this cultural step forward is far from complete. This is probably because the differences between individual peoples are in reality much greater than enlightened persons in a developed industrial society usually like to admit. The cultural progress we have been talking about has already been partly achieved, but much still remains to be done. It has as its essence that we should respect all people as fellow human beings, *despite* the manifest differences in humanity. Without this 'despite' there would be no need for progress, and the equality of fellow human beings would not have to be fought for.

Furthermore, racial or other discrimination against peoples or sections of a population often conceals economic motives. These motives seek to prevent people having access to wealth, or to take it away from them. So it is necessary to stretch the equality argument even further, to remove the pretext for discrimination. It should not be possible to exploit the very real differences between people, which in no way indicate different levels of humanity, in order to gain advantage in general economic struggle.

The progress towards enlightenment which I am recommending even in the community of mankind is far from complete as yet. This actually makes it easier to extend enlightenment beyond humanity. It remains to be shown that even in an area of manifest inequality, that between different living species, some kind of equality through affinity should be recognized. Enlightenment firstly lies in perceiving equality between human beings, as far as it goes, and drawing political conclusions for human co-operation. The second step, our becoming aware of our relationship in nature with the rest of the world, again lies in recognizing equalities despite manifest inequalities. I need not elaborate further on the differences which exist in nature; it is rather the elements of equality which require explanation.

Humanity's Kinship with the Connatural World in the History of Nature

Modern people tend to consider themselves as something better than nature. That is why the question of whether or not we are descended from apes was so offensive to the public in the nineteenth century. By now this debate has quietened down. For one thing, it has been a great relief that our existence does not have to be traced too directly back to apes, which are only a collateral line. Then in modern democratic society, origins are no longer taken as seriously in the formation of one's identity as they were in the days when one's parentage was the biggest determinant of the direction taken in life, and when in answer to the question 'Who are you?' the reply was to say whose son or daughter you were. All the same, it has become clear that in the end there is nothing we can say to refute the theory of evolution, and our inclusion in natural history, since it appears to be correct.

Several questions remain unanswered, though. Most important, is there a survival advantage in competition between individuals, and if so, whom does it benefit? And how far does co-operative behaviour fit us for survival? By definition, it is the fittest for survival who survive. However, we do not know what qualities and modes of behaviour make up this fitness, since the theories of selection which have been propounded so far are probably not the last word on the subject. But uncertainties of this sort do not alter the basic message of the theory of evolution: that humanity springs from the history of nature, as does human culture.

This is the starting point for extending enlightenment: that in common with millions of other species of plants and animals, the species *Homo sapiens* is part of natural history. In order to gain some perspective on the time relations involved here let us imagine that the cosmos began to develop just one year ago. The earth would then have been in existence for two months, the first large living beings (fishes) would have been on earth for ten days, and mammals for four days, although they would only have been widespread since the beginning of the day now coming to an end. The first hominids would have arrived scarcely one hour ago, and *Homo sapiens* would have been on earth for about five minutes. Wars, which according to popular opinion have 'always' taken place, would have been happening for half a minute, while the modern world would have been in existence for one second. Plants and animals are our relations in the natural world. In terms of time we are the newcomers, and our closest relatives are the mammals. Among them, the higher mammals are nearest to us.

In the past century there was a tendency to make assertions of the sort that humans were nothing but their physical components, that feelings were nothing but chemical reactions, and that illnesses were nothing but technical disturbances. A new variant of these 'nothing but' explanations is seen in today's sociobiology.[6] Nowadays it is genes which should be credited as the 'nothing but' in our ancestry: all life should be regarded as a contest of the genes, and organisms as simply their vehicles for survival. In the same way as its materialist precursors this theory gives a picture of society which, although it assimilates biological facts, neither embraces nor can be derived from biology. In particular, it is by no means clear in biological terms whether and to what extent human qualities can be assigned to genes at all, so that the theory completely lacks the biological basis claimed for it. In any case, it is interesting to speculate why a quasi-scientific theory of this kind should have aroused such an astonishing popular response. The reason seems to be that it propagates an egoistic picture of humanity which a good few people are glad to have stated in a scientific manner, connecting it with a view of nature which is correspondingly impoverished.

My point about humanity belonging to the natural order is different. Actually, such materialist interpretations of the world have not had scientific support for some time now, since quantum theory revealed matter as the manifestation of immaterial structures. On the other hand, it is no longer as a rule disputed that humans are organic, physical systems. No one who has been helped by scientifically-produced medicine can reject this recognition. Besides this, the physiology of human behaviour shows that our consciousness and our moods have a physical reality, and are susceptible to physical influence.

This kind of insight does not mean that our picture of humanity in terms of society and morality automatically agrees with scientific knowledge of our subjection to natural processes. As long as we are healthy we prefer only to recognize the social and moral identity, when we are unwell we have to accept the scientific; but their connection remains as open as that between health and illness. This is obviously true in a medical crisis, and it is equally so in the environmental crisis. We have not yet understood how physically we belong to this world; otherwise we would not be creating such havoc in our treatment of the connatural world and of our own bodies. To understand this better, we should now abandon the materialistic and mechanistic pretensions of nineteenth century scientific ideologists and their present-day successors, and this need not mean a decline in scientific standards.

'Our existence is physical.' Most people continue to hear these four words as five, as if they included the word 'merely', making the statement 'Our existence is merely physical.' This insertion is then countered, and replaced by another: our existence is not 'merely physical', but 'also physical'. So the two worlds once again fall apart, even though their linkage is by now crucial to existence. These insertions are steps back, taken out of fear that humanity is being devalued. This fear is unfounded: even the body itself is not 'merely physical'. Let us simply say that our existence is physical. This means humans belong by nature among the mammals, something that is repugnant to many people's self-esteem. But it also means that 'the nature of the whole has become human in us', and this could actually be a particularly good and promising development in natural history. The statement 'Our existence is physical' must therefore be understood in two ways.

Let us stick with the second one to start with. What it implies is that in the beginning of the world there was the chance of life. Heavenly bodies were formed, one of which is our planet. Our sun is among those which have not yet cooled down, and many others can be seen in the night sky. By virtue of the sun the beginnings of organic life emerged on earth. Photosynthesis formed an atmosphere containing oxygen, in which higher forms of life could also exist. All this took up more than eleven and a half months of our world year, but now everything was ready for the development of different life forms. The first fish came into existence, also land plants, insects, amphibians, reptiles, dinosaurs and the first mammals. After this came birds and the first primates. The dinosaurs disappeared again, while mammals spread. Finally came man; and then, only a second ago in terms of our world year, came a great event, a wonderful moment. *Homo sapiens*, the latest species to come into existence, stood up straight, turned his gaze on the whole, and addressed it as it is: as cosmos, ordered in beauty by virtue of the sun, a work of nature.

This was the beginning of our culture, manifested in the sun religion of the ancient Egyptians and the lucidity of the Greek mind. What an event in cosmic history! In one of these many million species – one equipped by nature with reason – the nature of the whole, the cosmos, so welled up in its own nature that it found speech, and expressed itself as 'physis', or later in Latin, 'natura', the existence of the whole, and of all that belongs to it. Was it not nature becoming flesh in us that addressed and recognized itself? In humanity nature attains language.

Nature, the life and being in all things, recognized itself through us in our environment, in animal and flower, tree and stone. It is we who have named them and we who can see how

nature's whole lives and blossoms in them, and how they belong
to the world and all have their specific value within the whole.
The world would be worse off, and the senses deprived, if there
were no sunflowers and no tortoises, no birches and no butter-
flies, no wind, no sun, no clouds, no sea. But we can also see that
not everything which came into being is beneficial. Almost all
life forms have something good about them, but a world without
the bacteria which cause malaria and smallpox would appear to
be better than one where they exist.

We can also see that with us in the world some things can
be more beautiful than they would be without us.

Was the variety of species in Central Europe at the
beginning of the nineteenth century not a product of agriculture, when this still was 'agri-culture'? In this climatic region,
instead of fields and heaths, meadows and pastures, there
would have been only a fairly monotonous forest. So can a world
with humanity in it not be more beautiful than a world without?
It is nature which is developing itself through us too, since we
come from nature, but with us some things can be achieved
better than they could be with only the elements and the other
species. This is uniquely true in the case of the arts.

Nature has endowed humans with such a variety of
abilities that we do no damage at all to our self-esteem in
recognizing the intrinsic value of other living beings and the
elements within the whole. Natural history might even be
structured in such a way that it is fulfilled in our doing so. A
requirement for this is our belonging to nature, the physicality
of our existence. Our physical being is that we are ourselves one
of the higher species, mammals like the others. This is the other
direction in which affirming our existence as physical counts.
We are an exceptional species, so special that we bring into the
world responsibility, hope and threat, in a way never known
before in the history of nature. But at the same time we are a
species like any other.

In our actions we must take account both of our common
nature and of our particularity. Our special nature within the
community of species is obvious, but what we have in common
with the others has not been sufficiently recognized so far. It

used to be the same in the relations between different races, cultures, peoples and sexes, until Christianity and later the Enlightenment led to the realization that all people, regardless of their obvious differences, are equally fellow humans. This step remains to be taken for our natural but non-human relations. Of course this does not mean that we should behave as we would towards people, when dealing with non-humans. Neither sunflowers nor elephants are human and however well intended it would even be offending their own dignity if we treated them as humans. Nevertheless there are points of correspondence, and the first ground rule of all justice, the principle of equality, should not be abandoned here. This means that we should give equal treatment where there is equality, and make distinctions where there are differences.

During the Enlightenment the equality of men was recognized in their identical birthright, as in the 'created equal' clause of the American Declaration of Independence. In a similar way, the modern state rests on the recognition of equality among individuals in their natural situation, in that regardless of any social differences each person is born to a mother, and brought up by parents. The fundamental principle of equality in birth can be retained in our relationships within nature, not in the 'born equal' form as with people, but in terms of equally being born. Having emerged from nature is what we have in common with other species, animals and plants, and even with the elements: the community of nature. Within this community our natural relatives, animals and plants, landscapes, seas, air and light, are our connatural world, or our fellows in the world, just as in our human community other people are our fellows.

Between humans and some parts of the natural world there is a still closer sense of equality in birth than is attributable to a common belonging to nature's whole. I refer to the higher mammals, which among all our relatives in nature come closest to being of the same family. This is readily understood in emotional terms. No-one can look a horse or a cow, a cat or a deer, or most of all an ape in the eye without being assailed by a particular feeling of being related.

It is not only justifiable, but essential, to treat different species differently, according to their similarities and differences: dogs cannot be treated like cats, or mammals like insects, or trees like ferns. Consequently, a system of natural justice does not imply the same rights for different species. Our feelings of kinship, whether close or distant, can help us to relate to other species as we do to each other where there are correspondences, and to mete out fair treatment appropriate to the similarities and differences. Even though we are only one of many species, self-consciousness implies the ability to be conscious of others so that we are not necessarily out for ourselves only. To some extent we are able to treat other beings fairly according to their kind, cats as cats, lime trees as lime trees, even granite in a particular way, acknowledging for each kind the dignity of its existence. So far we have developed this ability furthest within the arts, and least within the industrial economy.

It is intrinsic to our nature that we have the ability to ruin the very things we could make particularly good. Nature itself has achieved language in us, and we can empathize with other creatures; but the astonishing abilities given to us are perverted as we perceive everything only from our own angle, always putting that small word 'I' first. 'The eyes of all creatures look out into the open. It is only our eyes which are turned inwards, like a ring of traps preventing their free emergence.' Encounters with the connatural world can help us to extend our identity. It was, after all, a human being, Rainer Maria Rilke, who wrote these lines in the eighth 'Duino Elegy'. He continued, 'We are aware of the world outside only through the gaze of animals.' Humanity is not the whole, and nor is the connatural world; but at least it can reveal itself to us through the experience of living in interdependent fellowship.

Nature, Culture and Artefacts

What I would refer to as the connatural world is generally referred to as 'nature', though mainly as a resource, i.e. irrespective of its coexistence with us, and also in most cases only in the sense of the green world which is outside the window, or which is missed through its absence. Limiting nature to whatever is not human in the world has a long tradition. The opposition of nature to culture is contained within it, and it is true that human achievements in the world, particularly those which are cultural, had to be wrested from the natural order.

From the story of humanity's spread across the globe we can easily understand how nature has been considered as something alien, something to be overcome to gain room to live. The history of language reminds of this, since the Indo-European word 'rûm' (space) goes back to the concept of clearance by disposing of other environments, for a human settlement for example. In the intervening time we have taken so much of the earth away from the connatural world in order to serve our needs, that our environment has become oversized. The problem is now entirely reversed, and one wonders how other species can find room on the earth with human self-assertion at its present pitch. We have not been threatened by nature for a long time, but it is we who are now threatening nature. We need to understand both nature and ourselves differently, if we are to relate to the changed situation.

We can only escape from the threatening circle in which we find ourselves if we refrain not only from the wrong actions which endanger the basis of life, but also from the way of thought expressed by it. Here we need to recognize a distinction which was unnecessary earlier in history: that between the non-human world and the whole, to which humanity and the non-human equally belong. As long as there were relatively few humans and the earth as a whole was not given over to them, it was not important in human activities to distinguish between the whole, to which we belong as well, and the non-human world. Since then the position has entirely changed.

The great world religions and some major philosophical minds have long made the distinction that humankind must struggle against other species and the inhospitableness of the earth, but never against the world as a whole. On the contrary, humanity should refer itself to this whole, and should have a particular relationship with the rest of the world in nature's interests. So the Old Testament creation story teaches that humans must exercise dominion over their fellow creatures (the connatural world), and are held accountable for them to the Creator. In other words we are permitted to intervene in the world, and even should do so, but we are responsible for the effect this has regarding the whole.

I shall call this whole, the unity of all being, 'nature', and everything which belongs to it apart from humanity 'the connatural world'. In the environmental crisis it is vitally necessary to form the correct concepts and recognize the right differences. If we continue to limit the term 'nature' to what I call the connatural world, then the reality of our belonging to nature will fade even further. In the history of industrialization it was this mistaken understanding which prevented our consternation at the destruction of the environment from being converted into action. As a result, we have behaved as wrongly towards the rest of the world as we did towards the 'savages' in colonial days, taking no account of its coexistent being.

If we persist in excluding ourselves, we shall also be unable to articulate thought and action intelligently with respect to nature's whole, because the sort of conceptual framework we need is no longer found in religion. This whole, which is more than the sum of its parts, than humanity and the connatural world, I call 'nature'. It is the organizing principle in everything, animals and plants, mountains and rivers, sea and wind. These all belong to nature, for it is by virtue of nature that they are what they are, but none of them by themselves is nature.

In the environmental crisis, we must cultivate a new and revolutionary relationship with the connatural world and with nature itself as well. The distinction between the two allows us to put the questions in such a way that the answers may provide a guide for action. We are concerned with two different but related questions. For this reason I shall often refer to nature's whole, in order to indicate the distinction between nature itself and the connatural world.

The first question is how we should behave in relation to the whole, what it means to belong to it, and what we should

correspondingly do and leave alone. It is more important to me
to have the question addressed again than to answer it. However, in Chapter 4 I do give my answer: that there is no
contradiction between nature and culture, but rather that
culture is humanity's contribution to natural history. By this I
mean not only the arts, but also political and legal culture, as
well as the framework for an economy with rules in tune with
nature's whole, for example in a true agri-culture. If we bring
culture in this full sense into the world then a world with
humanity will be better and more beautiful than a world
without. That we can only create at the expense of creation is
a misunderstanding. Instead, we should be living for the sake
of creation.

The other question is how we should behave with regard
to the connatural world. Again, what is most important to me
here is that the question should once again be raised, so that
perhaps we will no longer unthinkingly let our actions be led by
the answer which dominates industrial society, that the non-
human world is there simply as a resource base for human self-
realization. Chapter 4 gives my answer to this question too,
that we should cherish the intrinsic value of the natural world,
and so even increase it within nature's whole. The additional
'within nature's whole' was missing from my book, *Ways to
Peace with Nature,* but is vital for the practicability of the
approach.

If culture is the human contribution to natural history
then it should give us the scale necessary to judge whether or
not things modified by human intervention belong to the
connatural world. Without thinking long we could perhaps
reckon that a tree would in every case belong to the connatural
world, that a house would not, and that in the case of a domestic
animal it would depend on how overbred it was. What is
common to all three is that they have been moulded by humanity, though not to an equal extent. In Germany, for instance,
forests are cultivated landscapes originally fashioned by G.C.
Hartig, H. Cotta and others, and there is hardly a tree in the
whole of Central Europe which, even if not deliberately planted,
does not owe its position to human approval. In addition, there

are many exotic trees in this country which do not actually belong here, except as adjuncts to human life. In spite of that, do they have the right to be considered part of the connatural world?

The case of domestic animals seems to be rather arbitrary too. Some of them, like sheepdogs and sheep, may look like belonging to the connatural world, while poodles and pigs with bodies so long that they sag in the middle do not. Even the third example, the house, is not as simple as it seems at first. If it is made out of stone, wood, clay or other naturally-occurring local materials it may resemble these more closely than the poodle does the wolf. Wooden doors to houses can look very much like the tree they are made from. Such craft achieves culture for wood, where trees as it were surpass themselves with human help. This moulding of nature need not stand in the way of naturalness, if culture is humanity's contribution to natural history.

So in deciding what belongs to the connatural world and what does not, general classifications or exclusions are problematical. The purist's solution would be to define the environment as 'natural' only where it is untouched by humanity. But such a definition would be of no help in the environmental crisis: the world around us demands attention precisely where we interact with it and ought to know what is happening, not where we have nothing to do with it. There are still some natural communities in Central Europe where life would carry on without humanity, in habitats like dunes, mud-flats and estuaries, freshwater margins, mountain tops, ravine forest and self-renewing beechwoods. However, most nature reserves are in reality man-made landscapes.

The other extreme would be to consider the whole of the physical world as natural. This would extend from the untouched connatural world beyond house doors and wooden houses to include rubbish dumps, motor vehicles and high-voltage cables, which would seem a little odd. Nevertheless this approach would have the advantage that we would then be dealing with the connatural world where we really have something to do with it. We see the products and riches of nature from animals and plants everywhere in the material world: wood from trees, leather from animals. Then there are stone and metals, and glass and such man-made substances derived from natural products. They are the reality of the natural world in our society, the civilized form in which we deal with it.

But can it really be true that the stone or clay, once part of the earth, which becomes material in the wall of a house, is part of the connatural world, while the wall is not? Is the tree felled for timber to make a house door natural, but not either the timber or the door? The wild plants which have been bred into cereal crops, but not the grain in its useful form? The wild animal within the domestic animal, but not the overbred species descended from it? Again, we are back to the position that the wolf forms part of the connatural world, while the dog does not; wild grasses belong to it while grain does not; wilderness forms a part while parks do not. The problem is once more transferred to an area beyond our concern.

We should not ease up in our search for the connatural world, even where we cannot find it, or where it is a sorry sight because of what we have made out of it. We can see the differences between a park landscape and an industrial area, between a wooden door and one made of chipboard, between a brick house and a concrete one. It is particularly important to identify nature where we have made an impact on the connatural world. Not to do so is an attempt to evade responsibility for our dubious actions. For instance, calves raised with hormones should not be slaughtered, but should be particularly well cared for until they die a natural death, to compensate as much as possible for the injustice done to them. That this doesn't happen shows how little different today's environmental policies are from the prevailing industrialism.

The differences to be seen between a normal and an overbred pig, and between a cultivated and a wrecked landscape, depend on how appropriately we relate with nature's whole. Where we have no need to feel ashamed, but can regard something moulded by humanity as part of the connatural world, we have brought culture into the world. When our actions have become doubtful, we should not escape from the question of appropriateness by abolishing the standard by which we make judgements. Quite the reverse: that is when it is most vital to see, and to make up for, what we have done to the connatural world within nature's whole.

Again, the question is more important than the answer. It does not follow that a course of action should necessarily be avoided because something will be destroyed as a result. Even in building a house very close to nature, trees must be killed and stones smashed. Before a stone or metal sculpture can be created, the earth must be ripped open and injured. If culture is the human contribution to natural history, the world cannot stay the same as it would be without people. In the environmental crisis it is entirely right, against the technological enthusiasm for change, to abstain as far as possible from the kind of destruction which has taken place up to now: but it seems to me that behaving as if we were not here could never make sense as a rule of life for humanity. But how far should we live at the cost of the life of other beings? How far do we act responsibly, and where does hubris begin? Where does destruction depart from culture? The two chapters which follow are devoted to these questions, and to such answers as can be given.

Notes

[1] Erdheim 1988
[2] Oviedo 1959, vol.1, 111
[3] ibid. vol.1, 118
[4] ibid. vol.1, 95
[5] Erdheim 1988, 34
[6] Dawkins 1978; Wilson 1989

Chapter 3

Responsibility for Nature

The concept of responsibility comes from the legal world. Everyone is responsible for what he or she has done, and can be brought to law for it if need be. The accused must then answer either personally or through an agent for the action taken and the intention behind it. The word 'responsibility' has its root in the Latin 'responsio', an answer – in legal Latin, an answer before the law.

People are not only responsible to others as individuals or as part of a group, but responsibility has become a structural principle of the modern legal state.[1] The idea that one can be called to account for the exercise of political authority is basic to the principle of the division of powers. This is less apparent in the writings of Montesquieu,[2] to whom the division of powers is a system of political balance, than in the earlier work of Locke,[3] who grounded his theory on the duty of office-bearers to be accountable to the public. Lockeian thought has had a marked influence on the modern legal state: everyone in a position of authority can be held responsible for the exercise of it.

How this responsibility should best be interpreted became the subject of a classical controversy, which has new significance today in the light of our responsibilities towards the natural world. Edmund Burke and Henry Cruger were elected Members of Parliament for Bristol in 1774. As is still usual today they made speeches to thank their supporters and to expound the task before them. Each had a very different view of what this was. Cruger explained to his voters that he wanted to serve them, submitting himself to their will, and being accountable to them in all his public actions. Burke countered that when a member is elected he does not represent only his own constituency in parliament, but is rather responsible to the population as a whole. 'Parliament is not a *congress* of ambassadors from different and hostile interests, which interests each must maintain, as an agent and advocate, against other agents and advocates; but Parliament is a *deliberative* assembly of *one* nation, with *one* interest, that of the whole ...'[4]

Both members recognized that they had taken on responsibility, but Cruger interpreted this as accountability to his own supporters, while Burke acknowledged a responsibility for the whole, the country; and although in any particular case he would justify himself to his voters, this would come later and was of secondary importance. Even if it is unconstitutional, Cruger's view has dominated in practice. Most politicians do not act out of responsibility for the country as a whole, but are guided by the justification they will give to the groups they count on for support. Who was right then, Cruger or Burke?

The difference between the two types of responsibility is that the first stresses responsibility with regard to oneself: the need to account for one's own behaviour, while the second takes on responsibility for other things and beings. Responsibility for one's own actions is orientated towards the past, since one only becomes responsible when a choice has been made and an action has resulted. By contrast, the way responsibility for other things and other people operates is in the future – through future actions. Responsibility of this sort exists only as long as the action still remains to be performed; afterwards one has either fulfilled or neglected it to a greater or lesser extent.

There is no need to make an absolute choice between the two types of responsibility. They each correspond to a particular time structure, and each has its justification. But the responsibility towards others in the future is of prime importance, since it precedes responsibility for the past, which operates only when responsibility in the primary sense has been missed. I would distinguish between the two by regarding the first as responsibility in its strict sense, and the second as accountability. Ethical philosophy of the modern era has mostly been preoccupied with how one should behave to have a clear conscience – as if our aim is to have a clear conscience, rather than to do what we are here for and what makes sense in our lives. The reference in Eisler's dictionary of philosophical concepts is characteristic of this view: 'responsibility – see liability'.[5] The definition under 'liability' deals with responsibility for an action or its consequences, culpability and accountability.

On the other hand in everyday language, as in the examination of human responsibility in the modern world, our future responsibility for other things and beings has come to the fore. Parents are responsible for their children, and only secondarily for their own behaviour, insofar as it affects the children. Should the need arise they can be taken to law if they fail to exercise this responsibility to their children properly. Someone who carries passengers in a car is responsible for their safety during the journey. The duty of accountability for one's own actions is derived from future responsibility and responsibility for others, and comes into operation only when an accident happens. So I do not consider accountabilities towards the connatural world. The question rather is, how far do we have responsibility for it?

Kant decided that it was just the other way round.[6] He thought that responsibility for something finally rested where we have to justify ourselves before others, and so, if we use my distinction, gives accountability a higher priority than responsibility for other things and beings. On this line of thought, someone who promises her neighbour that she will water his flowers has a responsibility only to the neighbour, not to the flowers, because they belong to him. According to this view she only enters into a position of responsibility with respect to the neighbour, whereas the flowers are a secondary concern. They are valued, but not for themselves, only as the property of the neighbour. Her duty concerns only him, not the flowers. It is as if she were watering him, not them.

There are probably only a very few people who feel that doing something for plants, animals or the landscape is not caring directly for them. But a relationship with the connatural world in its own right must be freed from a double distortion: we must get away from viewing the whole non-human world as the property of humans, and also from the traditional tendency to render every responsibility subjective, reducing it to individual accountability. The property question is addressed in Chapter 5, while the current chapter deals with responsibility.

Georg Picht posed the question of human responsibility in the modern world, which has been widely neglected by philosophers, and answered it as follows: 'Human beings owe the very fact of their existence to nature, and not just in physical terms. Nature's share in our existence increases with every level of mental development. The history of the mental development of the human race is the history of the mind progressively moving out into the realm of nature. History records the process of the mind's self-externalization.' Picht continued, 'Because historically human responsibility always refers to what is natural, this responsibility is not just for people, but also necessarily for things. In this age of science it has even become a responsibility for the preservation of nature as a whole. A definition of responsibility which leaves out animals, plants, raw materials, the water cycle and even the climate, because such responsibilities cannot easily be referred to the human subject, misjudges right from the start the essence of human responsibility. It should be repeated: having responsibility, man is a being whose identity is not defined from within but from outside. We become ourselves through history, mediated by nature; we become ourselves through nature, mediated by history.'[7]

It is remarkable that Picht saw climate change as a matter of human responsibility as early as 1967. In what follows I shall investigate why human responsibility does indeed extend this far, not just for the sake of humanity, but for the sake of nature as a whole. My theory moves through eight circles of responsibility, corresponding to an equal number of ethical systems. The first steps in this direction have already been taken by Frankena.[8]

Human behaviour is an expression of the way we conceive and appreciate ourselves. To understand the crisis of industrial society, now evident as a crisis in its relationship with nature,

I shall return to the self image of humanity which justified the rise of bourgeois society. The Old Testament myth of the Fall contrasted two natural states, the garden of Eden and the fight against thorns and thistles. Bourgeois society also harked back to a natural state, vividly portrayed by John Locke: a portrayal which legitimized that society.

Locke saw men in their natural state as free and equal individuals. The whole world, like America at that time, was a land to be settled, in which each individual could appropriate as much land as he was able to farm, without needing to take from others.[9] With the invention of money and growing population, people would come into conflict with one another; the formation of the political state was then necessary to protect property. This is the legitimation of the political power structure of bourgeois society.

Locke's picture of humanity is convincingly straightforward. Each person lives for himself and has as little to do with others as possible, or at least has no responsibility towards them. This is the ethic on which bourgeois society was founded. But it will become clear from its development that it cannot stay with it.

(1) Egocentricity – the Autonomous Individual

The free and equal individuals in the Lockeian 'natural state' exist for themselves alone. The circle of responsibility contains only the self. One takes care of oneself, and need do no more. In the state of nature Locke used to legitimize bourgeois society it is not in the least immoral to think only of oneself, so that the pejorative term 'egocentric' is actually quite inappropriate to this innocent self-seeking. All the same it is the word I shall use, since the fundamental principle of only looking after oneself lives on in the behaviour of the industrial countries towards the Third World, posterity, and the connatural world.

The division of the world into two by this circle of responsibility excludes any obligation to things and beings outside the self. For the Lockeian individual this definition is as narrow as

it could possibly be, with responsibility tailored precisely to
one's own body, including no one and nothing else. Each person
is responsible exclusively for him- or herself, and any dealings
with other individuals or with the world outside should be
handled in whatever way brings greatest personal advantage.
This theory of autonomy justifies such self-seeking, particularly when it comes to exploiting the outside world. Not being
responsible for others, and certainly not for animals, plants or
landscapes, the individual interest is to exploit everything
except himself. What lies outside the circle of responsibility
should be taken into account in one's actions, but only from
consideration of personal interest.

It is difficult to maintain Lockeian individualism for long.
A solitary human being is in fact not human, for 'you owe to
others what you are'.[10] The idea that society is a collection of
individuals is as absurd as the idea that a word is a collection
of letters. Individuals are moulded by their social surroundings; society can be divided up into them in the same way as a
word can be divided up into letters. To say that society is a
collection of individuals is to suggest that to begin with humans
were able to live alone, and only later grouped together. Locke's
individual would not know love, and language too only exists in
communication with others. Individuals who do not extend
their identity beyond themselves miss both love and language.
Hence the circle of responsibility should be drawn at least a
little larger.

(2) Nepotism – the Morality of the Clan

It is a short and realistic step to move away from the small,
independent 'I' by perceiving selfhood or identity as not merely
individual, but related to familiar others. Companions and
friends, relations and acquaintances, now find themselves
together in the circle of responsibility. This means that they
stand in relation to one another as they do to themselves, and
behave towards each other in the same humane way as they
would expect their companions to treat them. Identity is no

longer regarded as exclusively individual, but includes being partner, father, mother, son, daughter, friend and acquaintance of others.

Of course, to act towards others as to oneself does not mean to treat them in an identical way. A father does not treat his children in the same way as he would expect to be treated by them: individual differences have to be recognized within this reciprocal and equal treatment, so that fathers are treated as fathers, and children as children. But I consider that everyone in the circle of responsibility has reciprocal rights, so that not only is a father responsible for his children, but the children also have their own sort of responsibility for their father, even before they are adults. Actually most such groups of relations are in practice structured hierarchically rather than in the democratic way that would result from reciprocal responsibility. Otherwise the rule for this circle of responsibility – that a mutually familiar group feel a common and reciprocal responsibility for one another, and recognize each other's individual rights – is already quite close to the real relationships of solidarity in industrial society.

This widening of the circle of responsibility, so that one's own identity is perceived in relation to others as well as to oneself, is in itself a major step forward for humanity, a move away from Locke's solitary settlers. But things and beings which remain outside the circle will still only be taken into account to the extent considerations within the group require. This is true not only of the connatural world, but even of most of the people with whom we come into contact. Salesmen, teachers, politicians, drivers, farmers, policemen, livestock, grain and flowers, water and air, are required only for our own needs and the needs of the group, and there is no responsibility for any of them. The person who sells something is paid, and that is all. To the family the purchases are groceries or similar resources, but actually the trader is considered as a resource as well – as a resource for the supply of resources – while conversely he may consider the customer as a resource for earning a living. In turn, teachers are resources for the motivation and education of children, and politicians are resources for the representation of one's interests. In this sort of world, if something should happen to the postman, one expects the postal service, in its role as the resource for the delivery of letters, to send another in his place. What happens to the first postman would be a matter beyond the responsibility of those whose letters he formerly delivered.

It is not only family clans and mafia organizations which behave as if responsible only to a particular group, and stop at its interests and internal obligations in dealing with things and beings outside that circle. Such behaviour is common practice. Nonetheless, there are wider loyalties arising from the way industrial society sees itself. In the past, the next loyalty was to class. For both middle class and workers, the frame of reference was that of bourgeois society in the nineteenth century. The spirit of the times was bourgeois, and as a result even those who did not live like that class enabled others to do so by identifying themselves with bourgeois goals, upholding aims such as universal education which were derived from middle class society. The circle of responsibility was drawn around the bourgeoisie of the country. The rest of society and the connatural world were taken into account only where this was to middle class advantage.

The workers' movements succeeded in their aims to join the bourgeoisie, and a much more egalitarian society developed. Now a typical citizen answers the telephone himself, shops in supermarkets, eats a self-service hotel breakfast, drives himself around, and at home clears his own drains, perhaps with help from the neighbours which is later reciprocated. This type of consumer personality is still some distance away from connatural humanity, but democratic society at its best has a considerable republican quality about it, in the way common questions, *res publica*, are settled. This is done in a community of free citizens, without class distinctions, and in open discussion where everyone has a fundamental right to take part in decisions. We are on the way to such a democracy. It is now apparent that the social movements of the nineteenth century have led to a change in the character of our whole society, not only in the status of the workers.

The workers' movements were regarded as international from the very beginning, but despite this all without exception ended up confined to separate nation-states. These are the next stage in enlarging identity and responsibility in our attitude to the connatural world.

(3) Nationalism – Fellow Countrymen Unite

The circle of responsibility is now defined by one's own country or nation, a community of the same nationality, within which people treat each other as equal citizens. Such is the contribution of nationality to identity that we feel obliged to help if a fellow countryman met overseas is in trouble, for example. The sort of nationalistic pride that glories first and foremost in being French, German, Russian or American has traditionally been called chauvinism, and the term nationalism is hardly more approving. In fact, national identities have become obsolete to some extent, especially in connection with claims of sovereignty and the right to declare war, which should no longer be permitted in the age of atomic weapons. On the other hand, a national framework can create very useful loyalties, which scientific and technical progress should not be allowed to hinder.

The increasingly international nature of politics has led to some progress, and chauvinism is not as prevalent now as it once was in some parts of the world. But it has survived so well in international economic parlance that when an indicator is required for the well-being of a country 'the national economy' is chosen. In industrial nations, there is an awareness that individual economic interests are not necessarily those of the economy as a whole, so that at least in principle the economic health of a particular firm is distinguished from that of a country. This is also true for individuals in their contacts with each other, economic or otherwise. No one should act responsibly only towards friends and relations, for every citizen in a democracy also has a responsibility for the country as a whole. This principle is well enough recognized to impute irresponsibility whenever individuals, companies, or interest-groups deviate from the norm. But while some action is taken against this sort of irresponsibility within nations, there remains a problem internationally, which is not adequately recognized. What is usually described as the international economic order consists of an onslaught by the strong on the weak, and does not deserve the euphemistic term 'order'. Here individual countries and multinational companies battle only for their own interests, and might is counted right. The furthest-reaching irresponsibility at this level is the change in the climate resulting from industrial economic activity.

It is often said that we are all in the same boat here, as we shall all be equally affected. If this were really the case then attention to national interests would be all that was required to take care of international well-being. It would be unnecessary to think in a fundamentally different way, since what harmed the world would also harm us. We would be behaving in a way that was globally responsible, even when merely fighting for our own interests – trying to prevent adverse consequences as far as possible.

Such a theory is an illusion, enabling us to live a lie to our own advantage at the expense of the Third World. The industrial countries must recognize the plain truth: in global terms, and particularly towards the Third World, they have been behaving more irresponsibly than ever before. The early military wave of colonialism, when the Western countries first became richer than any others, was followed by a second economic wave, which continues to make us even richer. The future threatens to bring an 'eco-colonialism', the danger being that the industrial countries will continue to destroy the natural basis of the Third World.

Obviously, political change that does not benefit some more than others is scarcely conceivable. Even after it has become very plain what should be done, often nothing happens, the reason being that somewhere a particular interest group would either lose advantages or have to accept disadvantages. To give an example, levying a carbon tax on motor vehicles, a measure which is both an obvious energy saver and extremely easy to administer, meets with greater resistance from workers and pensioners who live in the country, and who often drive long distances, than from most other motorists. So how could we imagine that a change as wide-reaching as an alteration in global climate would affect all countries equally?

All political experience indicates that climate change will bring both winners and losers; we can expect nothing else. It may be that advantages and disadvantages will only be relative, in that, although all will lose, some will lose more, or even much more than others: these will be the real losers, the others winners at least in relation to them. Those who are unwilling to see that this will happen are creating an illusion of international solidarity, which can never exist unless further action is taken. Such solidarity could be built on insights into the regional, or distributional effects of climate change, if this were not prevented because recognition of these effects is taboo.

To work out the winners and losers, we must know what the consequences of climate change will be, and how they will affect different regions of the earth. Climate forecast alone is insufficient. In assessing the effects on living conditions in any particular country, we should take into account how much rain falls and how heavily, its distribution and its frequency, as well as the probable changes in climate variability such as an increase in hurricanes. It should then become possible to foresee how agricultural yields will change, how frequent drought years will be, how hurricanes will affect housing, how tourism will develop, and so forth. This is all largely unknown because research on regional climatic effects has started only recently; yet in spite of this the degree of unanimity about the global situation among climatologists is remarkable.

We can make certain assumptions even in our present state of knowledge.

(a)   Predictions of a rise in sea-level vary between thirty and fifty centimetres by the middle of next century, with a small probability that it might even be several metres. What is certain is that its effects will be different in different places. In Western Europe or the USA the investment volume of billions of dollars would give stimulus to the building industry, whereas in Bangladesh large areas of the country would simply become uninhabitable.

(b)   It appears that those countries which already suffer from drought will suffer even more under a changed climate. We do not yet know exactly. But it is certain that this is a major risk, and risks are harms too, affecting the very countries where drought conditions already occur frequently, where they do not have the power to combat such conditions, and whose economies are largely based on agriculture. Industrialized nations are not in this position, but many of the countries in the Third World are. How sensitive these latter would be to climate change has to some extent been quantified in a study by the International Institute for Systems Analysis in Laxenburg, conducted under the auspices of the UN's environmental programme.[11]

(c)   The Northern countries of the world are not as vulnerable as those in the Third World in agricultural terms, and it is certain that they will be less affected, so that they will derive at least a relative advantage. It is possible that they could even gain an advantage in absolute terms, in comparison with their present state, though this could happen only in the long run, and would certainly not be as dramatic everywhere as in Iceland, where the one hundred percent increase in the amount of carbon dioxide in the atmosphere presupposed in the IIASA model could increase the growing season by two months, and more than treble the pasture available in the country. We could also expect the northern parts of Russia, the USA, Japan and Canada to benefit.

There will certainly be winners and losers,[12] and according to all predictions the losers will again be Third World countries, since they are by far the most vulnerable to climate change. At the 1988 World Conference on Climate Change in Toronto, the threatened consequences of such change were compared to those of nuclear war. I consider that the number of people affected will be even greater. Who should be held responsible?

The culprits will be the winners. The northern industrial nations, both east and west, account for 75-80% of the cause of climate change, half of it resulting from the carbon dioxide produced by our energy-based economy. Chlorofluorocarbons (CFCs) and methane are each responsible for a fifth of the damage, while nitrous oxides and tropospheric ozone are also major factors. In short the causes originate in the material well-being of industrial societies.[13] The extent to which this prosperity is based on the exploitation of the Third World was in the past still debatable. It is now indisputable, in whatever terms, scientific, economic or political.

Ought we to be continuing with this lifestyle? Should the rich countries not now make a common declaration to the others? 'We, the rich countries of the world, are appalled to discover that we are maintaining our wealth at the expense of the living conditions of the poor, by causing climate change. We will stop using CFCs as quickly as possible, within a few months; we cannot deal so quickly with our use of energy, even with the abundant goodwill which we now possess, but we will reduce it by about a third within a few years. We will use intelligence and capital investment to harness alternative sources. We shall certainly be putting a stop to private motoring. Every citizen of our rich nations is happy to make a personal contribution to this effort. Our prosperity has been created on a basis of irresponsible action. It goes without saying that we shall attempt to give compensation for the damage we have caused, so far as this is possible.'

Sadly, no government has said anything of the sort; officially there has been unanimous silence on the subject until finally the Rio declaration acknowledged the industrialized countries' responsibility, at least in principle. Instead of speaking out, many governments have tried to quieten things down by saying that we are all in the same boat, and that we must wait for further scientific investigations. It is obvious that these supposed uncertainties are only a front, since basically climatologists have long been united in their views, which urgently require political action. Of course there are still open questions, but most of what ought to be done is required already from current knowledge. Also it is conspicuous that the countries which are keenest to bring up the uncertainties are those which look from our current knowledge of climate change as if they stand to gain, for example Russia, the USA and Japan. Besides, there is considerable resistance in the industrial countries to discussing the question of winners and losers, since it might result in paying compensation to the Third World. Criticism of population growth in the Third World is also used to create a diversion, although global environmental problems are overwhelmingly caused by those countries where there is no growth in population. Since the seventies I have feared that, in political terms, the imminent change in climate would be seen, or rather ignored, only as white chalk on a white wall; although I also expected that the critical point would not be reached, because of the enormous possibilities for saving energy. But from the winner-loser perspective I see that my argument is lamentably confirmed.

As long as political participants limit the circle of responsibility to their respective countries' borders, I do not see how catastrophe can be prevented. Sovereign states take no inherent interest in what happens on the other side of their borders, except as it affects the interests of their own country. Some day it may happen that hundreds of millions of environmental refugees will indirectly endanger our way of life. But will these not be fellow human beings? Should the world economy not recognize an ultimate common responsibility which transcends the borders of nationalism, and immediately too?

(4) Anthropocentrism of the Present – Fellow Humans Near and Far

If the governments of all countries in the world were to recognize a common global obligation, the circle of responsibility would embrace the whole of humanity, as one community. Each person would then be not merely an individual, nor just a member of a particular group or class, nor even a citizen of his or her own country, but a citizen of the world on equal terms among billions of others. The narrower, more limited identities and levels of responsibility would still be preserved, just as familiar responsibility is not removed by responsibility to the state, but is both embraced and restricted. In the same way as at the third level of responsibility it is no longer permissible to gain advantage for one's own family at the expense of the common good, at this higher level it is no longer permitted to exercise current interests at the expense of humanity.

How can many governments together assess international responsibility? If the general interest in future is to fit in with the national level of responsibility, then we must come to the founding of a world state, or at least a global power monopoly for conflict control. There is a danger of war inherent in a new and much greater social question which is developing internationally in the same way as it arose nationally in the nineteenth century. This is the contrast between the poverty of the Third World and the wealth of the industrial countries, who are to a great extent jointly responsible for that poverty. The greatest political task of our time is to develop, if not a world state, at least some kind of international solidarity, which will set the general interests of humanity against the egocentricity of nationalism. Recognition that development politics have failed because they were hegemonial politics of the industrial world will have to be combined with the understanding that north and south must now, as a first priority, create a new relationship with one another in global environmental politics.

Many people already see themselves primarily as world citizens, rather than, say, Scandinavians. Others are on the way there when they consider global threats which transcend individual states. Yet it is a high demand that one should ultimately recognize a duty to humanity as a whole, and not just to oneself, one's own circle or at most to one's own country. Even the well-meaning can end up in difficulties, for example when they meet one of their five billion fellow human beings abroad, without understanding a word of the local language, let alone the culture. We must first learn to feel a responsibility towards our fellow human beings:

– towards the people of Tierra del Fuego, whom we are endangering along with their environment because of the hole in the ozone layer;

– towards small farmers in Brazil, who are burning the Amazon rain forest, because big landowners are cultivating the land in the south to provide animal feed for Europe;

– towards all fellow humans whose living environment will be disturbed or destroyed by climate change.

Otherwise we shall not understand why:

– the use of CFC's must be halted immediately;

– we must ourselves no longer derive direct or indirect benefits in our economic dealings with the Third World from the destruction of tropical rain forest, as the enquiry commission of the German Parliament, 'Preventive Measures to Protect the Earth's Atmosphere', demanded in 1990;

– apart from phasing out nuclear energy, a widespread move away from burning fossil fuels is also required in the industrialized countries.

And how can all this become political actuality, if we do not even realize that it has to happen, and if humanity as a whole does not form a community of responsibility? As the environmental crisis is now global, there is no solution to it within the ethics of the nation state.

Looking beyond national borders has far-reaching consequences for more than the economy. From the viewpoint of the Third World, the climate issue is sometimes felt to be tainted with the same imperialism as before, and they are sceptical of what is put forward as a common interest, having been taken in too often over what the rich considered common. This reaction is only too easily understood, but it severely prejudices the interests of those countries affected by our economic activities. In an equally inward looking way, many critics of atomic energy in our industrial society do not recognize the climatic problem, which they regard as being fundamentally a propagandist argument of the opposing side. I believe we must halt our nuclear energy programme, but doing so presents more ethical difficulty than it once did. Regardless of who is for or against it, we are not entitled to evade a danger entered into nationally like this if by doing so we submit other countries to another danger, that of climate change. It is even worse to endanger others than to endanger oneself. Hence a rapid reduction in the use of fossil fuels is a higher priority than shutting down nuclear power stations. That is why I would only consider an immediate abandonment of atomic power – say within one or two years – to be justifiable if correspondingly greater efforts were made to reduce our emissions of carbon dioxide at the same time, in recognition of this priority. It is hard to imagine this happening, in view of past failures in energy policy, and because any such action could not be allowed to result in a greater burden on the natural world. This is a painful consequence for the critics of nuclear power. It is still possible to abandon it, but how difficult that may become depends on three factors:

– whether or not it is confirmed that a global reduction in carbon dioxide emissions of 20% by 2005[14] and of more than 50% by 2050 is not too slow;

– whether the richer countries decide to cut carbon dioxide emissions accordingly by at least 30% by 2005,[15] to compensate for the rise in emissions in the countries of the Third World;

– whether CFC emissions cease by 1995.[16]

Scrapping the atomic energy programme depends on utilizing all the options which remain after every possible step has been taken to avoid further climate change. Such options do exist, but there are fewer of them than there appeared to be before climate change entered into consideration.

It would be a major step forward if our circle of responsibility extended to the whole of humanity, with everyone behaving responsibly towards everyone else, so that no one could become just a resource for others. But the benefits of such progress would be restricted to humanity, with the connatural world still seen merely as a resource. The world picture corresponding to this circle of responsibility is anthropocentric: *anthropos*, man, stands in the centre, and the rest of the world is around and for him. The other species of the connatural world would at best find niches in our environment. Still, it would be progress if the anthropocentric ethic were actually followed in industrial society. But this ethic is not yet fully formed in the above discussion, because there is a step missing: in the words of an American Indian saying, 'We have not inherited this earth from our parents, we have leased it from our children.'

(5) Anthropocentrism – Humanity as a Closed Society

The well-being of the industrial economies is maintained at the expense of the Third World, posterity and the connatural world. We need a major shake-up in our thinking to give us the will to tackle climate change even if it only affects other people, as I hope I have made clear. The next step in realizing responsibility must be the inclusion of future generations. In any case, the argument for all humanity is bound to extend beyond the present generation, since climatic problems develop over decades.

   Consideration of future generations in economic activity is nothing new, at least in agriculture and forestry, as long as the tradition of sustainability is still relevant as an economic requirement. The responsibility we have to future generations, to those to whom we leave the earth, has come alive in public consciousness, especially through the revelation that our nuclear waste will last for thousands of years. Our descendants will have to live with the legacy of destruction left to them by today's 'affluent society'. Could we make up for this by leaving them cultural, scientific and technical achievements which will make their task easier in compensation?

   The circle of responsibility should now be drawn so that

those born after us have no less of a chance in life than we had when we were born. I shall not go into further criteria.[17] When we extend our self-awareness to include posterity it is a salutary exercise to try balancing the costs of our present affluence, as far as we know them, against the achievements that were handed down to us. To do so will help us to recognize how shaky the ground is under us, rather than selfishly believing that posterity will be happy to accept as genuine progress what are really only problems in the making.

Finally, if the dead are also drawn into our circle of responsibility, it will no longer be contentious to suggest that we should behave so as to take account of *everyone* else, of the living, the unborn, and the dead. The living would be responsible for the remembrance of the dead, and for the inheritance of those to come, and no-one would be simply a 'human resource', as human beings are conceived in economic terms, there only to serve external interests or those of a particular part of humanity. Have we now reached the very boundary of human identity, or being oneself? Is humanity a closed society? Certainly we do not belong only to one group in which all members are related either personally or by common interests, and most people in industrial societies nowadays do not find their fullest identity in belonging to a particular nation. But how sure can we be that by recognizing our membership of humanity, we have fully understood our identity as human beings?

(6) Mammalism – Higher Animals Unite

Humanity embraces all individuals, their partners, families, friends and acquaintances; all peoples, the living, the dead and the unborn. But why should humanity set the limits to its own identity, when being oneself has so far had to be redefined again and again, from a wider and wider perspective? A solitary human being cannot be human at all, but needs to interact with other people to become him- or herself. This basic fact has already led us to a series of further steps. Can humanity define itself in its own terms, rather than by referring itself to other beings? Is there not a more embracing whole, within which human identity, selfhood and responsibility could be more fully determined and embedded? Individuals who have no other yardstick for their behaviour than themselves are antisocial in tendency. Does this not also apply to humanity as a whole? Is anthropocentrism not simply a last effort to pretend that humanity, at least in its activities, is somehow better than nature, and so to justify our antisocial behaviour in nature, even after the acknowledgement that we belong to nature has become inevitable?

In the previous chapter I explained why humanity is not a closed society in biological terms. Our existence is physical, and because of our origins we stand in physical relationship to the connatural world around us. All species refer themselves to the other species with which they come into contact, through their frames of perceptual reference. Human beings especially have the natural disposition to consider their responsibility towards other species, because of nature's gift of reason. These other species again behave in their own ways towards humanity, not in terms of human responsibility and perceptions, but according to their own inborn capabilities – through cats' eyes, for example.

Our individual development is shaped by relationships, and not only with other humans. Language itself, the most exclusively human of our abilities, is first learned through association with another person, usually the mother. But this process implies developing self-awareness on the one hand and referring oneself to the living and inanimate things of the connatural world on the other. So language works simultaneously in three ways, referring the 'I' to itself, in identifying an idea as one's own; to other people, with whom one communicates by speaking in the same language; and to the connatural world, which the idea relates to. What is most human about humanity can only be known through living together with other people, *and* in relating oneself to the connatural world; not by confining ourselves to individuality, but by extending outwards to be with other things and beings. In using language, it is about as realistic to stick only to self reference as it is to build a bridge connected to only one bank of a river.

In our use of language we constantly relate to other things and beings. The threefold linkage between oneself, other people, and other things, emerges when a child stands up, recognizes space and discovers herself within it. It is no coincidence that the two basic questions people ask in the first couple of years are whether a child can talk yet or walk yet, for these two abilities are linked together in the same way as grasping something with head or hand. Approximately every fifth word we use is a spatial metaphor, as is 'metaphor' itself in its original sense of transposition. We do not merely live *in* space: human selfhood and identity, our whole being, are themselves spatial. To put it the other way round, the 'I' is only present in spatial terms, and can be lost in dizziness. 'In any kind of dizziness or giddiness our very being is overwhelmed, not just our spatial awareness', and 'on recovery one finds oneself again in all senses, not merely spatially'.[18]

We can only find ourselves in a spatial context. Space is the condition of togetherness, with people and with the connatural world. It is only within this co-being that we can recognize what we are, and that is why humanity cannot be a closed society. Not only does the individual only become a human being in being with other people, but humanity is in the same way dependent upon co-being with the connatural world. Self-awareness of the individual does not only refer to a person, and self-awareness of humanity does not only refer to the species. Humanity exists only in co-being with other things, with people, plants, animals, landscape and the elements. Without them we are not yet human.

Once our self-awareness is broadened to allow for our kinship with other species, the first we look to are the warm-blooded animals which are our closest relations in the animal kingdom. This relationship is evident in a positive way in our sympathy with them, but also negatively: very few people can bear to look at the way these animals are treated by industrial agriculture. This compassion is connected with the fact that like us they can suffer pain. So the circle of responsibility should be extended beyond humans to the community of all creatures able to feel pain. This goes beyond the anthropocentric ethic since in its frame even the higher animals exist only to provide food for humanity, so that factory farming is fully justified if good food is produced by the process.

This widening of responsibility to include the higher animals is different from earlier extensions. There cannot be a reciprocal feeling of responsibility between all the species which belong to it, since responsibility is a specifically human way of dealing with others. Reciprocity this time lies in living for others, we for them and they for us. I shall return in the next chapter to the question of how far our lives could justify demands on the lives of other creatures. For the moment, I shall confine myself to how as humans we should best relate to animals, so that humaneness is not lost beyond humanity. The practical difference, when animals are included in the circle of responsibility, lies in perceiving that they have intrinsic worth within nature's whole, and do not exist simply to provide us with food. Historically, there is nothing new in the idea that we should perceive animals in terms of their intrinsic worth; in ancient times Plato characterized the good shepherd as the one who cares about 'the best for his sheep', and not about 'the feast he will have, like a host preparing for a dinner party, or about the price he will get, like a trader'.[19] There is a huge difference between this outlook and factory farming. Even if animals were not only milked or shorn but finally eaten, they would at least have lived before they were slaughtered.

If we look back from the position we have now reached the anthropocentric picture of the world and of humanity is revealed as a kind of chauvinism, humanistic rather than nationalistic. This conception of the world had its most consistent philosophical expression in Descartes' dualism between non-spatial human existence and the merely spatial existence of the connatural world. Descartes defined the former as *res cogitans* – the reasoning part of the world – and the latter as *res extensa* – nothing but extended being. Through this unnatural classification of humanity and the inhuman classification of the connatural world, the human subject had lost its place in nature, even before the rise of industrial society, which conceived *res extensa* as an economic resource to fit the spirit of the times. That we no longer recognize ourselves in Descartes' theory is a further pointer away from the anthropocentric order of power and domination.

Reunion with the higher animals is something, but even at that rate the rest of the connatural world still remains merely a food supply for humanity and its kin. This is certainly better than anthropocentrism, but only to the level of what one might describe as a mammalistic ethic. Should we stop at this? Will it do to regard hares and mice as fellows in the connatural world, while trees and flowers continue to be regarded simply as resources? And what should happen about the destruction of the tropical rainforest?

There are many millions of species on the earth, perhaps five million, perhaps fifty – we simply do not know. 1.4 million species have been catalogued by scientists. It appears that the variety of species in tropical rainforests, of which the Amazon is the largest, is ten to a hundred times as great as in Europe. For example, there are about 25,000 types of tree there, including palms and lianas, compared to about thirty here. On one particular tree species, about three hundred species of insect have been counted, half of them being exclusive to that type of tree. So if the Amazon forest and the corresponding areas in Africa and Indonesia were destroyed, only a fraction of the variety of species on earth would remain. How can we welcome the higher animals into our company yet destroy all this variety? Once we were supposed to give names to the other species committed to our care. Now we do not know them, and cause their death. Species are dying out at a rate about ten thousand times as fast as they did before the arrival of man. The catastrophic extinction of species now looming has no parallel in previous natural history.

(7) Biocentrism – the Community of All Lifeforms

Albert Schweitzer's guiding idea was that, while we should not treat all living creatures equally, we should have great respect, or reverence, for the life in each of them, and behave towards them in a suitably responsible manner. 'Ethics means extending our responsibility unconditionally towards everything that lives.'[20] This definition is very much more obvious than limiting the circle of responsibility by drawing a line through the animal kingdom, so that only animals which can feel pain are taken into account for their own sake. Does suffering not reach further than pain? Anyone who has an understanding of plants knows that they are perhaps the most sensitive of all organisms, and that they can suffer as intensely as animals in their silence, although less expressively. The talent for sympathy with other living beings admittedly varies widely. It is rare to find animal lovers who are also plant lovers, and then there is a third group, who most easily relate directly to the elements: to water, clouds, air and winds, to light and gloom, to rivers, landscapes and seas.

The circle of responsibility is much more clearly drawn if life itself is now used as the criterion; but this does create an entirely new difficulty about the way we live off other species. From an anthropocentric viewpoint that was no problem, as long as cannibalism was excluded. But we cannot care for other beings as our natural kin and yet continue to dine untroubled. Vegetarianism used to seem like a way out. Most vegetarians make a clear and categorical distinction between animals, which they definitely will not eat, and plants, which they eat without thinking, as if these had no intrinsic value in nature's whole. I suspect that many of them are trying to escape from living at the expense of other beings' lives. But if we follow an ethic of respect for all life this escape route is blocked. To avoid living off either animals or plants, one can imagine humanity subsisting on fruit, milk products and vegetables which can be cut, and then grow back. That this is impractical for the present world population does not yet justify us.

Though he has often been accused of idealizing nature, Albert Schweitzer perceived this problem very clearly. 'Existence is hideously split by the will to live. One being wins through at another's expense, one destroying the other.' 'I am also subjected to this splitting. My existence is in conflict with that of others in a thousand different ways. The necessity to damage and destroy life is imposed upon me.'[21] There is no way, not even vegetarianism, of escaping the terrible fact that life as a human being is only possible at the expense of other beings' lives. We should have no illusions about being able to keep ourselves apart from nature's food-chains by not living off other species: we are so much a part of nature that we inevitably even share in the process of eating and being eaten. The more we can realize how nature suffers from this, the more we can recognize the expectancy, like St Paul in his Epistle to the Romans, that humanity may offer some signs of hope for the creation to be set free from the bondage of decay.[22]

Respect for the dignity of all life is an enormous step towards further overcoming human arrogance, once the decision to take the higher animals into account has led us beyond the anthropocentric ethic. At this point the circle of responsibility embraces all living beings, recognizing their individual rights and value in nature's whole. Together they make up the circle where we humans can achieve true humanity. Only the so-called inanimate world remains excluded. Respect for all living beings will not stop us from regarding this world as a resource for life, with no natural rights of its own. But is it really thinkable that the sea and sky exist only for fish and birds, and should not be taken into account for their own sakes?

(8) Physiocentrism – the Whole Round World

The previous extensions to the circle of responsibility moved from the individual to include family and friends, the nation, all peoples of the world, and humanity as a whole, including future generations. The final step was to look beyond the boundaries of humanity to include all lifeforms. Our responsibilities have now been widened to an almost unimaginable extent. It already becomes quite difficult for us to consider other species in our activities when the harm we are doing them affects us as well. Industrial society up to the present has not even gone that far. So surely it is merely Utopian to take account of other species

for their own sakes, and not only when there could be consequences adverse to humanity? But the environmental crisis
facing industrial society is so grave that only a Utopian idea can
now be realistic, and this is not yet complete. Up to now a
slightly broader chauvinism has always simply replaced a
slightly narrower one. Of course, nationalism is very much
more narrow-minded than anthropocentrism, and the degree of
arrogance inherent in respecting all lifeforms rather than the
cosmos which supports them is slight, and means that this time
the transformation is not so difficult. Yet the residual arrogance of one part of the world towards the remainder deserves
the name, and perpetuates a mistake which, though differing in
degree, is common to all seven forms of the progressive ethic we
have been examining.

Let us visualize the smallness of the biosphere within the
cosmos. Life as we know it is restricted to our planet, which is
scarcely a dot within the universe. Terrestrial life is purely a
surface phenomenon on the continents, and even in the seas,
since the maximum depth for marine life, eleven thousand
metres, represents scarcely 0.2% of the earth's diameter. One
can see how thin the covering of life on land is by looking at cliffs
or digging a hole, as the layer of humus comes to an end after
thirty to fifty centimetres. Life comes from the edges, where it
blossoms from the elements. But now what about these elements, the realm of life, land and sea, air and light? Do they not
belong like life itself to the circle of responsibility which is the
measure of our humanity?

The four elements are the script for life. A plant needs
earth, water, air and light, providing energy for photosynthesis, before a seed can take root and grow. When a plant
progresses from seed to blooming, we are actually seeing the
elements in bloom. Animal life in its turn depends on plant life.
The boundary conditions of all life are determined by the
elements. The encounter or association between air, light,
water and earth shows what these four can do, nurturing the
lively germ into full life.

Is it reasonable that the basis of life should not equally be
taken into account for its own sake, along with living beings?

Three of the four elements are today severely under threat; the earth through the poisoning of its surface, water through pollution of seas, rivers and groundwater; and the air not only from pollution, but from structural and dynamic changes such as the destruction of the ozone layer and climate change. The fourth element, fire, or light and energy, is not under threat as the sun itself. Here the danger derives from the fact that the sun's radiation is being excluded more and more from the energy budget of industrial society, and with different energy sources it is apparently less easy for life to grow out of the conjunction with the other three elements than it is with the established group of four within natural evolution. Do these changes affect the elements only because they make up the conditions necessary for life, or should we also consider them for their own sake?

When I am sailing on the sea and can no longer swim in it this saddens me, not only because I would like to swim, or because of the fish or other sea creatures, but for the sake of the sea itself. Whether it is gentle and still, or full of terror and menace in a storm, it has its own character and its own value. It is not just that we are polluting the water and offending against other living beings, by expecting them to live in filth and poison; we also sully the sea itself, instead of fearing and loving it. In it lie the origins of life, and reverence is due not only to what is brought forth, but also to that which brings it forth. For me, seeing a hedge without wild plants in or around it has the same effect. I feel sorry for the plants which are dying out, but also for the earth, which no longer has the chance to bring forth so much life.

It is more difficult to perceive the individual character of the atmosphere. It is the sun's energy which causes it to move, as the wind stirs up the water. But though waves cannot occur without wind, they are also the characteristic movement of water itself, roused by the wind, which is for its part the characteristic movement of the air. We experience how closely wind is connected to life, when it moves through the trees and blows the dead leaves back to earth. Even more than the sea, which is only calm when the air is, the atmosphere has the quality of stillness. It allows everything to pass through it; but when the sun's rays do so it becomes light and forms the sky above the earth. Without air the world was silent, no sound being transmitted. The atmosphere itself was in existence at the very beginning of life, and of the four elements is the most closely connected with development of life. Now the atmosphere too has been drawn into the web of destruction, this very atmosphere in which plants grow up towards the light and animals breathe, which has sheltered everything so that we have scarcely felt it. Is it only a loss to living creatures? Does the atmosphere in its own right deserve less respect than that given to the earth and the sea, or to this or that species? I do not think so.

The circle of responsibility is now so wide that nothing should be seen as existing merely for the sake of something else. One part of humanity does not exist for others, other species do not exist simply for humanity, and the elements of life are not there simply for the benefit of living beings. They all have their specific value in nature's whole, and all should be shown consideration in the activities of the species which nature's gift of reason has made able to identify this value. Within this circle, the yardstick for assessing human existence is no longer restricted to our being with other people or species, but is implicit in our treatment of the connatural world as a whole. Man is not the measure of all things; all things coexistent with us are the measure of humanity.

Notes

[1] Saladin 1984
[2] Montesquieu 1748
[3] Locke 1690
[4] Burke 1774/1975, 158
[5] Eisler 1930
[6] *Episodischen Abschmitt 4* 'Metaphysik der Sitten'
[7] Picht 1967, 328
[8] Frankena 1979

[9] Locke 1690, 49, 29, 36
[10] Goethe, *Torquato Tasso* 106
[11] Parry et al. 1988
[12] K.M. Meyer-Abich 1992
[13] German Bundestag 1989
[14] the 1988 Toronto recommendation
[15] German Bundestag 1990
[16] German Bundestag 1989
[17] cf. Birnbacher 1988
[18] Dürckheim 1932, 403-5
[19] *Republic* 345cd
[20] Schweitzer 1923/1974, vol. II, 379
[21] ibid. 381/387
[22] Romans 8, 19-22

Chapter 4

Foundations for a Holistic Ethic

The expansion of the circle of human responsibility, from total self-centredness to acknowledgment of the intrinsic value of the connatural world within nature's whole, is linked to a corresponding expansion in self-awareness. Anyone who follows these ideas through, not as a mere hypothesis – a little exploratory stroll – but by not returning to the starting point, is a different person at the end, and a changed self-image will express itself in changed behaviour. In moving from one level to another, one does not only change in oneself; it is like being born into a new world.

Relating to the World

If I perceive myself first as this body alone, taking care of myself does not cease when I identify myself secondly as the son of my parents and part of a community of others besides, and behave accordingly. Thirdly, through a further extension of awareness, this expanded identity is embedded in attachment to my country, so that consideration for myself and my personal circle does not permit me to offend against public interests. In turn, I shall recognize fourthly my responsibility as a world citizen, no longer prepared to follow national interests at the expense of the international community of peoples. This identity as a world citizen is extended a fifth time when I recognize myself to be a human being more generally, owing my identity to both the dead and future generations. The anthropocentrists consider at this stage that they now know what they owe to others, and what life should really be based on. Whoever perceives the sixth progression, that humanity is not a closed society, and in recognizing the seventh realizes that animals and plants are our relations in the natural world, will know himself or herself for 'a living being with a will to live, among other living beings with a will to live'.[1] Now it will no longer seem right for a human being to act in ways which damage the biosphere. The eighth and last step is to experience the nature of the whole as our own. Now all previous identities are subsumed in this one, and care for the whole takes precedence over all other considerations.

This ever broadening understanding of the human personality with the wider definitions always including the narrower, corresponds to the wholeness of human existence in the world, which began with mere spatiality. One lives not only in one's own flat, but also in the block to which it belongs, in the street to which the block belongs, in the suburb of which the street is a part, in the town of which the suburb is a part, in the country of which the town is a part, in the terrestrial zone of which the country is a part, and on the earth itself of which the zone is a part. The wholeness of a town can be judged by whether people feel as much at ease in it as they do inside their own apartments – by whether they feel at home in it. Today we need to feel that the whole earth is our home, and so our identity ends neither at our own front doors nor at the borders of our own countries.

Caring for one's own interests is possible in many different ways, depending on how far the sense of belonging to the world extends. Working outwards, one can understand oneself egocentrically, nationalistically, anthropocentrically or physiocentrically, but contrary to a widespread belief, not solely anthropocentrically: egocentric thought has not even reached the anthropocentric, while the physiocentric goes beyond it. A simpler and more usual distinction which is generally made is that between egoistic and altruistic behaviour. The two cannot be so sharply separated however, since altruism is a way of being oneself as well. The Christian command 'Love thy neighbour' is not to behave altruistically, but instead to love others *as ourselves*, in other words, relationship with others is ultimately connected with selfhood. One cannot respect others and exclude oneself, or exclude others and care only for oneself. The holistic system of layers, in which we to a greater or lesser extent care for ourselves, and finally at the eighth level care for the entire human and connatural community as we do ourselves, refers all relationships with other things and beings to the perception of one's own identity.

Some people may feel, in view of the present state of human self-perception, that it is expecting too much to be at once able to care for the world in the all-embracing way the foregoing conclusions have led us to. Would it not be a major step forward if humanity, which up to now has stuck to national interests at best, would just consider the entire human race, even including future generations? This would not imply any philosophical objection to the argument for thinking in physiocentric terms, but would rather be a pragmatic moderation of the radical philosophical idea. I cannot approve such moderation for political reasons, since although clearly everything cannot happen at once, the necessary steps can at least be begun simultaneously on all eight levels of responsibility. In general it will be necessary in future to think and act in the widest possible terms, whereas the narrow environmental politics which has been attempted up to now, has hurried from one disaster to another, giving rise only to partial, if not merely symbolic, actions, without consideration for the whole. It has been like building dykes only in front of villages.

Thinking beyond the boundaries of one's little self may well have been slightly easier when the earth still appeared to be the centre of the universe, and when if we humans did not actually form the centre, at least we lived at it. For Plato, to care for oneself was to think cosmically. The movement of the human soul ought to comply with that of the heavens, where we might observe the circuits of celestial intelligence and take them as a paradigm for the kindred revolutions of our own thought.[2] Those for whom this was too high flown should at least refer themselves to the earth in their own terms; like shepherds, for example, who should take care of the sheep for their own sakes and not only in expectation of milk or roast meat. The loss of the geocentric world view through the Copernican turn which initiated the modern era has made it very much more difficult to think outwards from oneself in such an all-embracing way.

But in politics one can also make the mistake of not believing in people enough. One should have no illusions, but those who simply declare that the world is wicked and behave accordingly make it even worse than it is. In politics, without hope we are lost. In order for the world to become better we must believe that it is not hopelessly ruined. It has been ruined, yes: but not hopelessly. Without a belief in people even democracy would not exist.

The Christian knows that 'By the grace of God I am what I am',[3] and in other religions too people find themselves in God. The secularization which resulted from the Copernican revolution means that in the modern Western world this support has been progressively lost. Instead of looking for the paths of life as 'labourers together with God',[4] conceiving the world as created through Christ,[5] moderns have been restricted by an anthropocentric view of the world. Thinking beyond oneself now meant thinking beyond the individual, beyond one's own family, situation, class or nation. It has not even meant caring for humanity for a very long time, as history from colonialism in the Third World to the climate crisis shows.

The path which enables us to think in a broader way even after the loss of the geocentric and Christian world views is that of reason. This is Immanuel Kant's approach. He also distinguished the things of nature, which are governed by natural laws, from the nature of the whole, to which these laws correspond. According to Kant, it is this one nature which has 'added reason to our will to govern it'.[6] Reason is a gift of nature, which is not only human nature, and it is through this gift that we recognize the moral law. 'Act as if the maxim of your actions could be transformed by your will into a universal law of nature.'[7] To act in this way is not an externally imposed obligation, but our own will led by insight; it is as if we had given ourselves the law from within. So we find through nature's gift of reason a measure of our humanity which is not merely human. To consider our own interest then means to consider not only our own interest but, by virtue of reason, the interest of the whole of nature as it expresses itself in reason, nature's gift to humanity. Kant also described what might be the natural course of human history in his *Idea for a Universal History with Cosmopolitan Intent* (1784).

Interpreting Kant in this way may seem unusual to some people, because in his practical philosophy freedom was found only beyond the material world. Following contemporary science, he saw things physical as subject to natural laws, and not to be included in the realm of freedom. The stumbling block is confusion between things *of* nature and nature *itself* – rigidly separate in Kant's definition. Being must not be confused with that which exists by virtue of it.

The idea that someone who 'listens to nature' may be granted a reasoned insight into the order of the whole, or 'logos', stems from Greek natural philosophy.[8] Kant did not contradict this, but rather emphasized that reason is a gift from nature to *humanity*. Every concept which we grasp is thus anthropomorphic, humanized, just as, according to Uexküll, what is seen resembles the eyes which see it. It in no way follows from this that we must also think in *anthropocentric* terms, not taking the connatural world into account except when human interests in any sense below that of level 8 are at stake. The difference between the two is like the difference between the personal and the egocentric in individual behaviour. Whatever a human being claims or does will be personal, but not necessarily anthropocentric. Where Kant himself thought anthropocentrically we should not follow him, but nor should we turn our backs on his insight into the anthropomorphism of human thought and the aim of determining the human will from nature.

The answer to how far we need to think beyond our immediate concerns is very different now from what it was in Kant's day. In his time, it was important to inculcate responsibility to all humanity. The Prussian mind was receptive to this idea. The nationalism which arose with the French revolution formed a major setback, but nonetheless the modern legal state has codified new recognitions of common responsibility. Each responsibility which is not purely individual requires a general consensus, with many individuals joined in identifying with it and recognizing it as a common responsibility. Where today do we find acknowledgement of the common responsibility the industrial countries have towards the Third World? Or of common responsibility for the connatural world coexisting with us? We behave as if carrying out these responsibilities were not our business. But it is the essence of democracy that citizens do not want to shift common responsibilities into the hands of kings and emperors. Then, of course, such responsibility falls on the global community, which must reckon with it in both personal and political terms.

Aristotle understood man to be 'by nature a political animal'.[9] He saw our political motivation, that is our acknowledgement of common responsibility in our life with others, as a natural ability. *In humankind nature becomes political.* The political upheavals of the modern era have led inexorably to the foundation of the modern legal state, though admittedly only in parts of the world. A revolution for nature should move us towards the wider community we need to create before we can deal with the global implications of the industrial economies, which reach far beyond the organizations of single states. The goal of this revolution is justice for the whole, or peace with nature – peace of the parts with the whole. In us nature attains language, in its terms we think beyond ourselves, and within us it becomes political. But whether nature takes up or misses the chance of freedom inherent in humanity depends on us.

It is not a new idea that humanity gives us solidarity not only with all other humans, including those in the Third World, but also, in the essence of our being, with the connatural world. As Novalis states, 'I do not know why people always talk of humanity as something apart. Do animals, plants, stones, stars and skies not belong to humanity, and is humanity itself not simply a junction of nerves, where different threads are endlessly crossing? Can we understand it without nature? Is humanity then so different from the rest of nature's stock?"[10]

Experiencing nature in the physical world must be connected with experiencing the same unity and entirety within our human nature, so that we can feel at home in the world as a whole. We can only fully experience the nature of the outside world, when we experience it equally as our own inner nature. This means recognizing the connatural world as we do ourselves, while at the same time in our recognition allowing ourselves to be recognized. This is the agenda of an alternative science. We also only truly experience our own inner nature when we rediscover in it the nature of the physical world.

The unfolding of the circles of responsibility revealed the holistic structure of the human personality. This bridges the gap between the level of common humanity recognized by the modern state, and the wider concept, which includes our coexistence with the connatural world as part of our humanity. We are not merely individuals, sons or daughters, and national citizens, but beyond that world citizens and members of the community of nature or of the whole. This whole is not the sum of all those beings which have a part in it; rather they are what they are through participation in the whole. This is true in a different way for human beings than for cats, sunflowers and seas, but it is equally true for all of them. We are genuinely thinking and acting in our own interest only when we accept global responsibility for nature, as our own nature.

It is the basic concept of my father's holistic philosophy that the parts are determined from the whole, as 'simplifications' at different levels.[11] For a living being to have an environment in Uexküll's sense means 'nothing other than to be part of a more embracing whole. Actually wholes always exist within other wholes'[12] When the human personality is equally integrated with the social and natural environments, being conceived as more or less all-embracing, then we have an ethic and a political philosophy to suit the physiocentric world picture. To go beyond our responsibility as citizens of nations, perceiving our global responsibility for peace with nature, is to fulfil our natural, human political bent. This fits the pragmatic approach to holism, as a 'philosophy of political man'.[13]

Culture: the Human Contribution to Natural History

The physiocentric world picture which should replace the anthropocentric allows everything, living or inanimate, its own dignity within nature's whole. It is not a return to the geocentric cosmos of antiquity. The centre around which everything revolves is no longer the earth, but the whole.

It seems like a tall order to recognize everything's intrinsic value, without allowing human selfishness. If everything which exists must be respected and guarded as it is, do we not have to hold ourselves back from making any change in the world? How could we feed ourselves? In the end even a sculptor would not be able to transform a stone into sculpture, for then the stone would not remain what it was. And would that not deny its intrinsic value, or dignity?

It is not possible for us to leave the world as if we had never been here, and it is certainly not humanity's part in natural history. Quite the contrary: why are we here, if not because a world with human beings *ought* to be different from a world without? In my opinion, the view that we should avoid as far as possible making any change is completely wrong. I can easily understand how many people have growing doubts that humanity may be expected to bring anything good into the world, when they see the destruction the connatural world has suffered at the hands of the industrial nations. Yet I cannot come to this conclusion myself. What is more, although we have been changing the world over the last two hundred years in a way which cannot be allowed to continue, I see no reason for resignation. The mistakes we make are so stupid that after careful consideration nobody should conclude that we could not do any better.

Philosophically, there are two things to be considered, if we are not to give up in view of past failures, or to take comfort from the supposed inevitability of anthropocentrism. Firstly, all things and beings have intrinsic dignity, not simply in their respective individuality, but within nature's whole. It is nature which forms the centre, not the single being or species or type, and this is true for everything, not only for humanity. If humanity really cares for itself only when caring for the whole of nature, the same is true for all other things and species. Every being is in its own way as great as the whole world, like a monad, since each owes its being to the whole.

Secondly, there is the point which I used as a basis in Chapter 2, that the natural interconnectedness between all living species and things is a historical one. Nature has a history, a past and a future. It is pushing itself towards something which is still to come. Creation is still to come; it is not over and done with, and it will be going on for a long time. Novalis said, 'God is nature's goal, with whom it should come into harmony one day.'[14] Nature develops, and the result will be what it really is. I think that as humans we should contribute towards this process. How far a species or thing as it now is has fulfilled its historical potential, or whether it could fulfil it further, thus remains open not only for humanity, but also for the rest of the natural world. Aristotle rightly recommended as a rule that 'we should seek for nature in whatever is natural, and not in what is corrupt'.[15] We can also use this rule to consider history beyond the present situation. The intrinsic dignity of things and beings within nature's whole is revealed as what they can *become,* when the whole fulfils itself in their particular being: it is their nature, the paragon of their better possibilities, in other words their entelechy. To respect everything for its intrinsic value is the principle of a physiocentric ethic, and every present situation is to be assessed with respect to the future.

Science can describe the direction natural history has taken up to now. Its starting point, which has been extrapolated cosmologically as the Big Bang, was arguably the most boring episode in world history, so uniform that as yet nothing could be distinguished from anything else. In the course of billions of years from this uniformity, an almost eternal and ever more beautiful and various cosmos has developed, and on our planet there has evolved a variety of life which is correspondingly rich. This happened by itself, through nature. By its creative power the universe developed itself into galaxies, light and dark, heaven and earth, land and water, mountain and valley, animal and flower, tree and stone, and finally into humanity. 'With gentle pressure and counter-pressure nature moves to and fro, and in this way here and there, over and under, and before and after come into being, determining all the phenomena we meet in space and time.'[16] Nature perpetuates itself with everything it brings forth, including us, as Goethe says elsewhere.[17]

The general scheme of this development is the continual creation of new forms in increasing variety. But there are also setbacks. Since about the time of the industrial revolution this variety has been decreasing, because humanity has lived at the expense of the conditions basic to life. Most seriously, the economic prosperity of the industrialized nations since the Second World War has led to a rapid and continuing species extinction unprecedented in natural history. Even without human interference, there have always been downturns in the general development, particularly during the ice ages, but these have not been so sudden or so wide-reaching. Nature does not necessarily perpetuate itself in the optimal way. Forms of life are not necessarily well-adapted; they are merely better adapted than those which have become extinct.

The facts of natural history, as far as we know them, hence do not help to assess the climate changes we are causing compared with those of earlier history. It would be a false conclusion to suggest that further climate change can be justified because changes in climate have already occurred from natural causes. What is happening now, as the majority of all species are destroyed at one go, has probably never occurred before. However, the development of the natural world up to this point cannot be used to determine whether this is right or wrong. So where do we find a measure for human behaviour?

It is not as difficult as it appears to find an answer to this question in philosophical terms. Again it is essential that we must not confuse the one nature, the whole, of which we are also a part, with the connatural world, the non-human part of the world. Current epistemological theory holds that the laws of science are not to be inferred from the experiences of the senses. Rather, we are able to recognize them because, in Kant's famous dictum, reason brings them forth according to its own design. This recognition is possible because reason is the voice of nature moving to and fro in our thought, the way in which the nature of the whole attains language in us through the principles leading human knowledge. This is not only true of science, however. Reason is also the living voice of nature determining our will, in the communion of the soul with itself.

My driving motive is the conviction that in us nature is perpetuating itself the human way and that how far it succeeds depends on us. Those who unlike me consider that industrial economy has been rational, and that a holistic ethic is irrational, are also impelled by driving motives. Their motivation should be as openly expressed as my own. As far as I can see the destructive rationality of industrial society has an emotional and at bottom religious basis, involving suppression of thought about death. So the rationality of technology, in armaments and in civil industries too, has advanced so far that the deathly nature of its aims has been pushed out of sight. I am no longer prepared to accept this way of thinking as reasonable. The revolution for nature outlined in this book is certainly not directed against reason. On the contrary, reason must be won back to the side of life.

If nature attains reason not only to determine our knowledge but also our will in dealing with the material world, what does it have to say to us? How definitive can the answers we expect from it be? The Kantian programme in theoretical philosophy was only partly fulfilled for natural science within two hundred years. The necessity of developing a practical philosophy of nature, evaluating our actual behaviour, has only really been recognized in the present environmental crisis. Conventional practical philosophy, like politics, has hardly got past the third circle of responsibility, and in only a few instances has it gone beyond anthropocentrism. A practical philosophy of nature is still in its infancy. In this chapter I offer for discussion my own approach to a foundation for a holistic ethic. In what follows I refer to different fields of activity: nutrition, art, work, and the economy in general.

Food

'Come in, the gods are here too', said Heraclitus to the guests who came across him in the kitchen. More than that, the subtlest philosophy isn't worth much if it doesn't stand up in the kitchen. This criterion is crucial to a practical philosophy of nature, since it refers to the only form of activity which we could not give up except at the cost of our life itself. For this reason my starting point is the actual physical existence in nature of a species that needs to eat and drink, which is what we are.

The way we feed ourselves is the touchstone of a physiocentric ethic, and the basic issue of a practical philosophy of nature, because that is where we live off other forms of life. Living off one another is one of nature's organizational principles. We belong so thoroughly to nature that we too, in common with all living beings, must live off the world around us like our animal relations, at the very least by killing or injuring plants. We are dependent on other beings, and take at least what we need to live. What is the debt we owe for this? I do not see how we can escape this question. The rule: you owe to others what you are, also applies to the connatural world we live off. And when we recognize that we are dependent on something, but know that dependencies are always interdependent, we have to conclude that there may be something dependent on us.

There is scarcely a more archaic form of contact with the connatural world than taking something between one's teeth, biting, chewing and swallowing it. This unavoidable reliance on nature may lead to the belief, either complacent or desperate, that if we all have to live this way, how far we go with it is no longer important. It makes as much sense to conclude that as we have to die in any case it does not matter how often we risk death.

The question of what we owe for living off other living beings can also lead to the theological answer, that an existence with this determining factor is inherently culpable. I do not consider this to be wrong, but in that case how should we deal with the guilt? In my opinion we owe it to the plants and animals on which we live to eat them with gratitude and joy, rather than munching away in remorse, and compounding the guilt further. 'The meaning of physical life is first of all found in the fulfilment of the inherent claim for joy.'[18] Joy in eating and drinking, in love, clothes and holidays: such joy with pleasure but not only as pleasure might even be the key to renewal of the industrial society. As Fontane says in the *Poggenpuhls'*, 'Don't think that God made the world out of peevishness.'

When these joys become actual in us, are they only our own, or is joy brought into the world with them? A flower in a garden or a field is beautiful, but is a world where a few cut flowers decorate a dress or a table not even more beautiful than one where flowers are found only in gardens or fields? Might it not even be that the intrinsic value of some flowers is realized in just this way, in decorating that particular dress or table? And is the pleasure only ours when radicchio, zucchini, endive, tomatoes and peppers, with virgin olive oil and herb vinegar, come together in a salad? They would not be combined like this without humans to bring culture into the world in this and other ways. Is a world where such magnificent salads are found not perhaps more beautiful than one without? I shall go one step further. Does it perhaps contribute to the beauty of the world and not simply to our pleasure, not to mention our nourishment, when a fish is beautifully prepared and then eaten? Is the fish here only the pitiful victim of our life at others' expense, or is nature's particular purpose for the fish not perhaps also fulfilled by some fish being transformed into joy and pleasure at a celebratory meal?

I know that all these questions are a little daring. It seems as if I am going the way of justifying anthropocentric behaviour within a physiocentric world view. How do we now reply if somebody says, 'Well, if that's the case, I also gain pleasure from my car, and so I might even agree to a physiocentric ethic.' My reply to this is that I am not considering private convenience, but whether the sovereign reason, when it determined the direction of my will could share my joy, even with the fish. This is not anthropocentric, as far as man is not taken as the measure. For a critical assessment of the joy given to us, through the company of others, through plants in a salad, and through the fish, we only need to consider what happens after the meal. Let's assume that all waste products are properly used. What further behaviour derives from our joy in the gifts of nature? How are we to make a world with human beings better and more beautiful than one without? Or when we prepare a meal carefully, are we only balancing for ourselves the ugliness and destruction which we otherwise bring into being? Anyone who is nourished by eating the fish, but afterwards acts so as to prejudice the future existence of that or other kinds of fish, cannot possibly justify the fate of the fish even through the most cultivated cooking.

If we turn from what happens after eating to what goes on before, it is obvious that we cannot take pleasure in everything we eat. People who eat factory-farmed meat or eggs, saving money at a cost of animal suffering, can have no real joy in the food. That price is too high; no celebration can be based on such food. Appreciation of milk products and eggs depends on the way the animals are raised. The price of animal suffering is too high whatever the financial saving. Meat-eaters also should in principle be prepared to slaughter all the animals they eat themselves, and to vouch for the way it is done. The Jewish rule of eating only meat which had been drained of blood sprang from the idea of giving life back to the earth with the blood of the animal, before the meat was eaten[19]. Even though blood is no longer regarded as the epitome of life, this rule is still a very wise one in its basic assumption, that the quality of a meal depends on the previous fate of what is eaten. The same is true of plants. They do not suffer in quite the same way as animals in industrial agriculture, but nor do they fare much better. It is not only vegetables, fish or meat that are put on the table: they all have a history which is served along with the meal. It is only when their lives before being cut or slaughtered have been such that they have had fair treatment from us that we may ask in eating them what further obligation we have. Otherwise we should not eat them at all; we should rather liberate them so that they have at least a little compensation.

The behaviour of other species offers a few stimuli for secondary questions. It seems that they are unconcerned about what they owe for living off the connatural world. In their adaptation they follow the right course, which we have to search for, paying their debt unguided and unconsciously, since knowledge is not a part of their nature. In biology these relations were traditionally described as purpose. The natural historians of the eighteenth century were filled with enthusiasm for the wonderful organization of the natural world, where each species, while living its own life, is at the same time living for others. That we humans are not cutting much of a figure in this natural structure of interdependency if we live at best for a few of our own mates, has not been a theme of practical philosophy until now.

Art

Next to food, art depends on an encounter between the senses and things around us which is almost equally direct, but less problematical, because, as a rule, no living beings are hurt or killed for the sake of a work of art. The criteria of such encounters are again sensory, and provide a chance to draw beauty into ethics at last.

Thought becomes physical in humanity. In us thinking has become a natural process, like the flowering of plants and the movement of animals. It can be passed on through language, so its embodiment in artefacts such as books is not essential for its existence. The fine arts operate differently. By its very nature, a work of art cannot be complete as a mere thought, although that is very much part of it; it also requires a physical existence outside the human body, not necessarily a unique one, although that too is true in many cases.

Colours are obtained from organic or inorganic materials. Plants must be made into canvas, or woods into boards, before a picture can be painted. The trunks of felled trees are sawn and chopped so that a carving can be created. Stone is quarried and ore melted into metal for sculpture. These interventions are almost insignificant compared with those of industry, but is the fact that they seem permissible only a question of scale? If something is destructive on a large scale can it be completely harmless on a small one?

Art is quite different from the industrial process. When industry abstracts something from the life cycles of nature, it only 'apparently awakes new life in them and at the same time sucks out its essence, until it decays into lifeless rubbish and is thrown away'.[20] Art on the other hand awakens the things in which it becomes material to a truly new life, enhancing the earth's richness. This is most obvious where materials are not used simply to represent other physical things, as with oil colours in a portrait. Even here the artistic achievement lies in the way the material qualities of colour have been transformed into a face. But this is easier to see if the observer is not distracted by the representation of a third object, and the material of the picture is in itself awakened to a life it otherwise did not have. Take, for example, cement in the earlier pictures by Tápies, hessian for Manzoni, cardboard for Schoonhoven, colour itself in its very essence in the paintings of Albers and Rothko, or in its light and haziness in Calderara and Erdmann.

In this sort of art, no alien life is breathed into the materials, making them flare up and then sink to ashes. In a way, rather, they are being brought to themselves, in a fashion which nature could not usually accomplish without humanity. The same is true of sculpture. Nature makes bones without human help, but not Moore's sculptures, and surely a world with these in it is more beautiful than one without. Felled tree-trunks can develop a particular beauty of their own beyond death, but wood sculptures like Hans Steinbrenner's would never occur naturally. The sculptor Brigitte Matschinsky-Denninghoff has pointed out to me that pyramids are natural forms in the Egyptian desert. But the royal tombs of the Old Kingdom could only have been created by human hands.

In all these examples, it is noteworthy that the works of art, although they are artefacts, look natural, but in a way that nature would not have brought about without humanity. Art liberates nature, redeeming it from the incoherence which it still suffers. Of all human activities, art is the area where I am least doubtful that nature perpetuates itself with us, and so in art we fulfil our destiny. Not every work of art achieves this but some do, and the chance to achieve it is always being renewed. Art is a human contribution to natural history, in which we give something to nature in return for living off the natural world. Adorno thought that 'Works of art accomplish what nature seeks in vain to achieve – they open their eyes'.[21] However, he burdened the apt metaphor with the wrong antithesis, for it is nature which opens its eyes through art and perceives itself. In art nature becomes aware of itself through the senses, as it does in philosophy through the mind, having brought forth human-kind in which it has for the first time addressed itself as what it is, as *physis*.

The physical embodiment of works of art provides the purest encounter between humans and other beings, not aris-ing from desire or necessity, but bringing the natural world to a manifestation of itself beyond what it would have achieved alone. The purity of this contact in the approach to art has a cathartic effect on the human soul. As nature becomes aware of itself, so we become aware of it as being our own nature. Art is the form of knowledge in which this is possible.

On the other hand the approach of classical physics and of those sciences for which it became a paradigm is intrinsically intended to lead the way for technology. This is independent of the subjective awareness of the scientist, who often possesses no interest at all in 'applications'. Natural laws are forms of power, and if a hypothesis does not prove to be such in experi-ments it is rejected. If we compare the contrasting attitudes of art and science to the connatural world with attitudes to fellow human beings in colonial times, Oviedo's outlook, which I quoted earlier, corresponds to that of science. The approach in the same period of Bernardino de Sahagún (1499-1590) was in sharp contrast to this.

Sahagún was not concerned to legitimate Spanish colonial rule as Oviedo was, nor to question it as Las Casas (1475-1566) did. What he wanted was to allow the foreign culture to speak for itself, an aim which has by now become the ideal of ethno-logical research. To this end he first learned the language of a Mexican tribe that he wanted to study. But he did not begin to talk with them immediately: first he asked whether they actually wanted to talk to him. After thinking about it, they told him they were willing to do so, if he would return at a mutually convenient time. There subsequently followed talks and conversations which lasted for years, and these were recorded in *both* languages and scripts.[22] The tribe Sahagún questioned would probably not have been able to give such an account of its own accord. But external intervention should not go further than encouraging self-expression from the foreign culture. The artistic relationship with the connatural world corresponds to this approach to the human world. Goethe led the way for an alternative science to follow the example of art in this respect.

Work

Living off the natural world is more in tune with life the more it follows art, but it involves considerably wider-reaching intervention in the interdependency of life than art itself. In Third World countries economic activity as a rule consists predominantly of agriculture. In industrialized countries the agricultural component has sunk to only a few percent. What are the aims of the rest of the work done there?

In our present style of industrial economy, exchange of capital is many times that of material assets. The development from a production economy to a money economy goes far beyond alienation from work, as Marx perceived it. Accordingly, earnings become the overriding goal of work, rather than the transformation of materials into the necessities of life. But natural philosophy must finally assess even the most abstract sort of work in terms of the concrete transformations caused in the connatural world. I shall therefore concentrate on this question only. What sort of dealings with things and beings in nature can be justified, not for food nor art, but for the sake of the utility values of industrial civilization.?

The first chapter of Stifter's 'Indian Summer' has something to say about this. The young Heinrich Drendorf explains that in general he did not like it, 'when someone changed an object into something different from what it was. It particularly offended me when in my opinion the change seemed to be for the worse. It grieved me once to see someone fell an old tree in the garden and cut it into large blocks. These blocks were no longer a tree, and since they were rotten no stool, table, cross or horse could be carved from them.'[23]

In other words:

– Something should only be changed when there is a good reason for it.

– Each change is the metamorphosis of something which already exists, and which already has its own dignity, into a future form.

– If something is changed it should become better than before in the process.

– It can become better not only through art, but also in the transformation into useful objects.

What should be considered as 'better' within the framework of a holistic ethic is the theme of this book. In what follows I shall put forward some criteria for testing out the economic process in the light of this ethic.

The validity of Stifter's point of view is not confined to art. There are in any case connections between art and utility. Artists, particularly painters, usually resist any suggestion that their work might have a use; with some justification, they fear a narrow understanding of having to be useful if they once admit it. All the same, I believe this risk should be taken, because it does the development of utility objects no good if there is a gulf between them and art, so that they escape any artistic judgement. The beauty of a tree is not depreciated by the fact that one can eat its fruits. And surely we regard the Egyptian pyramids, Romanesque churches, the Doge's Palace in Venice, Michelangelo's square in the Capitol, Palladio's villas and the like as works of art? Looked at the other way round, I consider it a very worthy goal of town planning to build a town which is a synthesis of the arts, with scope for the art of living itself, and that the economy as a whole ought to be given the same orientation.

If proper consideration is given to nature's whole, towns must be harmoniously integrated into the landscape, which in turn must be altered to allow the town's embedding. The park landscape of Central Europe, as it still looked in 1800, is a good example of the way landscape even in its natural development can gain from cultural modification, if culture is regarded as the specifically human contribution to the history of nature. Without humans Central Europe would have been largely covered by beech forests, and the increase in biodiversity since the last ice age would have been far less than that fostered by agriculture, when it actually *was* 'agri-culture'. The cultivation of rural landscape in England tells a similar story. And in city gardens, the connatural world can develop aspects of itself which would remain dormant without human interference; though to achieve this plants need freedom to grow different from human designs.

Admittedly gardens and cultivated landscapes only occur because people decide that some species may live there and others not. This is not just a question of associating plants, but also of protecting some plants from others. Ground elder in a garden is and remains a thing of the devil. And should I not get rid of the greenfly from my roses somehow, if they are not eaten by ladybirds or their larvae?

Leaving gardens and landscape aside, the intrinsic dignity of the connatural world would be best served by what one might call a Socratic economy. By this I mean an economy which would produce its goods in the way Socrates termed 'maieutic', that is, like a midwife assisting at a birth. Products would be valued within the whole to the best of human ability. That raises the problem of what we should do to alleviate the birth pangs of this system. Apparently, the economic process is linked to the cultural transformation of the connatural world in a different way from the intellectual process in Plato's dialogues. Hans Christian Andersen described the pain inherent in development in his fairy tale, *The Flax*.

The flax grows in the field, blossoms, and thinks to itself (as we understand it, so the flax participates in our consciousness) 'This is fulfilment! How beautiful I have become!' Then the reaper comes, and the flax is terribly tormented, until it finally ends up as woven linen. And then, after all this distress, it occurs to the flax that this woven linen, in which it joins with other companions to form a beautiful fabric, perhaps represents an even higher fulfilment than blossoming in the field. But this stage does not last either, for the fabric is cut and sewn, which again is extremely painful. Out of it is made a magnificent dress, which is worn with joy and delight. The transformation was stressful, but is it not better to be this garment, rather than material kept in a chest? The dress is worn often, and so the flax too, but finally it is cast off and left in the wardrobe. Even if this were its whole life, it has come a long way. It is not finished, however: one day the whole process starts all over again, and what comes next is even worse than the making of linen. The flax has never experienced such tearing, such heat and such crushing. Finally it becomes paper, a wonderful large sheet of white linen-based paper. Is this not much better than anything which came before? But the history is not yet at an end. A book is printed on the paper. Once more comes the dreadful process of cutting and pressing, but with what a result! White paper is certainly a very fine thing, but the printed page is the carrier of thoughts which are much finer and greater than the paper they are printed on. Is this not quite simply the very pinnacle of fulfilment?

There is one final stage, and here opinions divide. When the owner of the book dies the book is thrown out of the window and burnt. One reading would be that the whole process was all in vain. The other, which is mine, and possibly how Andersen saw it, would be to ask whether ascending in light and flame, scarcely affected even by gravity, is not even better than paper and words?

Transformations like those in Andersen's fairy tale are not always the result of human actions. When a bird eats a midge which gives it strength to fly, the midge is transformed into the flight of a bird, and this is as light and transitory as a flame. The bird draws life from the death of the midge. The death of the midge must be regretted, in spite of the beautiful flight of the bird, but not mourned after.

In the same way as we should lock into the food-chains of the connatural world around us so as to cause as little destruction as possible, we must find a model for the corresponding chains of transformation in economic matters, and Andersen's story can provide one. The key elements in the story of the flax are that the plant grew naturally and blossomed by itself, and that things are revalued after the loss of their previous value. Moreover Andersen describes the transformation of the flax as the continuity of a whole life, which in its ripening goes far beyond that of the plant's fruit, and which is inextricably linked to the pain of development. Here we come again to the question of what we owe to the plants and to nature as a whole which gives them their worth, when they suffer from human economic activity.

Andersen ascribes the pain inherent in every transformation to its subject, the flax, which still survives even in the book, but describes it in such a way that it can become our own, and that is what matters. What is spent is cut down and transformed in such a way that something new comes into being, but without the pain of transition the renewal is no move into the future. Compared to this lesson, studious research into vegetable suffering during life, or even after death, would seem relatively trivial. What is important is that we should participate ourselves in the reverberations of the original pain of being torn from life, rather than trying to assess it outside ourselves. The 'work of pain'[24] which is part of human life must also embrace the connatural world, if we and it belong to each other.

Limitations of the Market Economy

The industrial economy is far from Andersen's sensibility in its dealings with the things of nature. If it possessed it, I would not have needed to write this book, which is itself a metamorphosis of trees I sadly did not know, but that hopefully once at least had the chance to live. Goethe saw long ago, in a discussion with Eckermann, 'a time coming where God no longer has any joy in

(humanity), and must engulf everything in order to bring about
a rejuvenation of creation'.[25] He could have thought that there
was quite some time to go, but today things already appear
quite different. We should not wonder at this. In our society,
and particularly in economic institutions, the most successful
man is typically the one who acknowledges no measure for his
actions, except himself in the smallest possible frame, the first
of those discussed in the previous chapter. This was not always
the case, but it has a long history, to which I can only refer in
a cursory fashion here.

It is characteristic of this history that the departure which
began with the crusades in the first century of this millennium
was continued in the voyages of discovery and conquest round
the world, which for their part provided the model for the
triumph of natural science and technology. It is unjust to call
the middle ages dark and unenlightened, when the vision of a
world of intellectual and political openness, with humanity
awakening to create it, was one which matured in this period,
and I am not at all sure that at the end of this millennium we
are any further forward in this respect than at the beginning.
It was a vision of truth and candour, with the clarity and light
of Greek reason, which we are now threatening to fall back
from. But from the beginning there were strange indications
that this might happen.

In the thirteenth century the monk Roger Bacon had a
vision of how a new experimental science would lead to the
invention of weapons which could kill from long distances
without any contact between the opposing sides. In this way, he
thought, pagans would be convinced of Christianity's superior-
ity. This was seven hundred years before the invention of the
neutron bomb, and four hundred years before the founding of
modern science. Since the fourteenth century, patrons had
gradually begun to be seen honouring the sacred personages in
religious pictures. This was not necessarily bound to develop
into anthropocentrism: it might simply have inspired their
successors to comparable gifts of devotion. But the patrons
began to take up ever more space in the pictures, approached
the diagonals, then went beyond them, and finally the sacred

entirely disappeared. In this way human beings moved to the centre. Eventually, in the seventeenth century, Francis Bacon (1561-1626) declared that a hidden way back to the paradise from which we had once been driven could be found through science and technology.

In the modern economic state humanity was to become the sole measure of all things. Adam Smith could hope that an invisible hand would direct the autonomous subjects of this economy, preventing them from making themselves richer at the expense of others or the whole. But the only corrective was lingering tradition, and that could no longer prevent the exploitation of fellow humanity in the early industrial period. In the environmental crisis, this economic selfishness has again driven industrial society to the brink.

Formerly communist countries are even closer to catastrophe in the present environmental crisis than free market economies. Their economic collapse offered them considerable scope to do some proper groundwork, but it looks as if this chance will be wasted through complacency and short-sightedness. This means that there is once more a threat of destruction at least as serious as that which accompanied economic upturn after the Second World War. Just at this time of environmental crisis, the selfishness of the market economy has set itself up as utterly absolute, posing as the source of life, and eroding the foundations of human existence like its own. This process can only be stopped by a revolution for nature, refusing to continue such destruction.

Unfortunately, it is the western industrial economy's greatest virtue, its adaptability or flexibility, that makes it blind to the abyss. As long as the economy is unconstrained by any outside frame of reference, it will recognize no measure other than itself, and external disasters will not even be perceived. There is continual adaptation, but only in the interests of internal coherence, regardless of what it may lead to. The virtue of adaptability has become an ability to adapt to the wrong way. Even in environmental crisis, there has been pressure to adapt so as to profit from existing conditions, not by avoiding destructive processes, but rather by using good management to squeeze new profit from the aftermath of destruction, for example by recycling rubbish profitably rather than by cutting down on it. A particularly paradoxical instance is the industrial breeding of plants, or perhaps even of forests, which are resistant to environmental pollution: this is being discussed in preference to stopping the actual pollution.

The external measure to be applied to the economy is how it integrates into nature's whole. It must be recognized that everything in the connatural world has its own intrinsic value by virtue of the whole, and must not be squandered simply as a resource. To this extent the crisis in industrial society is a crisis in its relationship with nature. Reintegration with the whole must be mediated by society. Individuals and peoples must once again incorporate their economic activities into the web of life. This process begins by finding a completely new orientation in our dealings with the connatural world, which must replace what we had before. It would have been better if we had followed an insight ascribed to Novalis from the beginning: 'If humanity wishes to make a step forward through the arts of organization and technique in its mastery of the external world, then it must first have made three inner steps towards an ethical deepening... If these three inner steps are not taken before the one outside, the so-called step forward will in the end cause only unutterable misfortune.'[26] We are already a long way down this road, and things are threatening to become worse, but even now we could find the strength to deepen our ethical base.

I have been considering our dealings with the connatural world in terms of food, art and work. The common denominator in all this is that *cultural* determinants must be brought to bear on the economic process. The economy must be bounded by goals and restrictions which cannot be justified economically, providing a cultural frame of reference for deciding what is an economic success and what is not. What will be the real costs of products which are apparently cheap? Choosing culture as the measure of the economy's 'social costs'[27] in the widest sense, has the attraction that historically economic activity has cared for and protected the natural environment best when it has also been cultural activity. This happened most obviously in traditional agriculture, though that is not to say that it did so without imposing long-lasting changes. If we abandon the standards we have attained at a high and as yet unpaid price, it is still possible in principle to rediscover options for economic activity which retain peace with nature. That is how things were done in the past: we only need the will to do so again. This means we must be convinced that the goal is right, and then it will not be so very difficult.

The present sense of the word 'art' is almost synonymous with culture, but though we do sometimes speak about the circumstances of everyday life as 'arts' – the art of food, the art of homemaking – the term 'culture' is generally restricted to cultural events, activities and institutions, to the fine arts and music, to museums and theatres. Such a narrowing of the field fits all too well in today's industrial society. However, if the economy is to be embedded and incorporated in culture, we need a broader understanding of the term. Culture can no longer be confined to 'cultural' events: it is the fabric of living, and nothing should be left out of the cultural sum. Technology and art have been developing side by side since the beginning of the modern era, and culture, to which both belong, would be the right frame for relating them to one another again.

It is not only the economy which needs to be reintegrated with culture. In humanity's dealings with nature, the sciences too have scarcely been viewed from a cultural standpoint for about a hundred years. This is because the branches of knowledge known since the nineteenth century as the humanities have been sidelined compared with the scientific and technical disciplines which are bound up with progress in the industrial economy. The humanities, to survive, consolidated a subject area of their own which concentrates on the inner self, the individual and history, and left the outer world to the scientists and technicians. This was understandable, but it has led to the connatural world being left totally at the mercy of industry and technology. By completely neglecting cultural mediation of attitudes to nature, the arts and social sciences have ensured that industrial dealings with the natural world were removed

from their cultural framework. Even in the environmental
crisis, the humanities' share of responsibility has recently been
denied through the so-called 'compensation theory', according
to which the humanities should make destruction more bearable, by making it the object of wit, without doing anything
about it.

The cultural weakness of our society appears in politics, as
well as in science and economics. Most seriously, forming
opinions about what sort of scientific and technical knowledge
industrial society should have in future is left by the public to
experts, although this implies preliminary political decisions
about our future way of life. Books such as this one are a
contribution from the philosophy of nature to a consideration
which affects everyone: what our criteria should be for evaluating how in future a world with people can be better than one
without, in biotechnology, energy technology, agriculture, chem-
istry etc. This discussion must be a public one, for what is better
or worse affects everyone, and everyone must know about it if
industrial society is prepared to become really democratic.
Reincorporating economics in a cultural framework is a question of political culture as well.

Culture in its wide sense, in its provision of a social
framework for the integration of politics and the economy in
nature's whole, is the very mark of the human environment.
The quality of this environment should be measured politically
and economically, and by the social reality of nature in the
processes of culture. Culture is the way nature moves forward
through us; it is what humanity brings to the world, which
would not otherwise appear in the natural community.

One of Max Ernst's pictures is called 'Mother Nature
Wearing a Wedding Dress in a Plum Tree'. Without knowing
the picture one might expect to see a woman in a wedding dress,
sitting in a tree as an allegory of nature. But the picture shows
only a tree in bloom. Mother Nature lives in everything, in
animal and plant, tree and stone. Through her presence in the
plum tree, the blossom is her wedding dress. Her presence in
humanity is manifest as the culture we bring into the world.

New life is always blossoming as other life fades away.

Just as dying and death are inherent in the healthy life of an individual, they are also inherent in every generation of individual species, and in nature as a whole. In Heraclitus' words, 'These live in the death of those, and those die in the life of these'.[28] There lies the hope that in the course of the world dying is not the end, since whatever dies lives on in those who are given life by that death, and ultimately shares in the life of the whole, like the midge in the bird's flight. The change between death and life with its inevitable suffering is recognized as a natural destiny handed down in the very earliest maxim of Western philosophy. This comes from Anaximander of Miletus (c.610-c.546 BC.): 'That from which beings come into existence is also that to which they are destroyed, in accordance with necessity. For they give one another justice and recompense for injustice in due course of time.'[29]

The concept of right within the community of nature's whole has recently been revived.[30] The laws of nature's movement, which we call natural laws, must be reconnected with the moral laws of human behaviour if the rules of human action are to fit into nature's order again. I shall not explore in detail the import of this for today's world. It can be shown that the former must be more than merely acknowledged, while the latter must be more than merely wished for, but that truth and common assent link the two. The following section is a series of propositions suggesting how an industrial economy could be restricted by cultural limitations in the interest of peace with nature, if we had the will for it. Accepting these propositions would necessitate an about-turn for the economy and a total change in lifestyle for every one of us.

24 Steps to Changing our Lifestyle

(1) Our task on earth is not to leave the world as if we had never been there.

(2) A world with people in it should be both better and more beautiful than a world without.

(3)   In the environmental crisis it is important to live wholeheartedly for this goal, not comforting ourselves with resignation to its impossibility.

(4)   Nothing in the world exists only for others. All things and all beings have intrinsic value which should be taken into account.

(5)   All things and beings have intrinsic value not only in themselves but within nature's whole.

(6)   Nature is historical, and this means that things and beings have intrinsic value for their fulfilment in history, which may not yet have been reached. This value lies in what nature may become in them, in the realization of the whole within their separate existences.

(7)   Reason, the living voice of nature (logos) within us, is a gift from nature. It is the way the nature of the whole attains language, through our motivation towards knowledge as well as through the human will, towards action.

(8)   Reason must be won back for life, and must not be claimed for rational paths which have deadly ends.

(9)   A practical philosophy of nature deals with the conditions for peace with nature, and so is crucial to the direction of environmental politics.

(10)   The crucial point of this practical philosophy of nature is that we live off other life, even so being a part of nature, and that we are therefore unable to escape the question of what we owe for this.

(11)   Because we live off other life we owe it to nature to eat with joy, artistry and festivity; to use the strength food gives us to contribute our share to nature's whole; to let the living things we eat have lived well before they are slaughtered, in this sense living off 'healthy food'.

(12) Art allows nature to attain language for its own sake, and for this reason is the sensory action through which we can best justify humanity's living off other life within nature's whole.

(13) Art wakes the things in which it becomes actual for nature, in a way that could not happen without humanity.

(14) Each economic action is the transformation of something which already has a value into something else.

(15) When there is no sufficient cause for change, things should be left to their own processes of transformation.

(16) When something is changed it should become better than it was before. This is possible even in economic activities, if monetary value is estimated on the general basis of what counts as better and more beautiful within a peaceful relationship with nature.

(17) The more artistic an economic action is, the further we can discharge our debt to nature.

(18) The cultivated landscapes of traditional agriculture are one way the natural world can be improved by economic activities, while another is towns which grow out of and blend into the landscape.

(19) Whatever is removed from the connatural world for use in the economic process should be received as a gift from nature. The previous history of any economic good affects the value it can have.

(20) Each item continues to have a value, even when it has lost its usefulness in its present context. There is a requirement that we should recycle.

(21) Recycling should be carried out so that the original gift of nature is nurtured into continuing life by whatever industrial process it undergoes.

(22) The connatural world around us should be economically managed under conditions which render the pain of transformation bearable. To be able to judge this, we need to sense this pain ourselves. Virgil's 'lacrimae rerum'[31] belong to grief for creation and of creation, through the nature of existence.

(23) The economy must have external aims and laws imposed upon it, giving it a cultural framework for measuring what is an economic success and what is not.

(24) Nature moves itself forward through us, in our bringing of culture into the world. Culture is our contribution to natural history.

In Search of Lost Nature

The economic process is far removed from art; but the more a product is a product of culture, which is the contribution we owe to nature, the nearer it comes to art. The concept 'art of life' expresses this orientation. As a result economic activities fit better into their cultural frame, and so into the life of the whole, the more they follow an 'art of life'.

The fine arts are a model for how we should root the economy in nature. When works of art appear natural, this does not derive from the realistic representation of natural objects, but rather from the way art brings the naturalness of the connatural world into the human environment, representing things in a different form from the one already assumed within nature; this means that the 'natural' status of art works is not derived from the connatural world, but from the naturalness of their own existence. Sculptures by Moore, Serra, R. Long, Matschinsky-Denninghoff and others do not imitate natural objects, but they are very much natural, and belong to nature in a way which nature would not have developed without humanity. In them is characterized the particular way humanity belongs to nature and shares in its creative force. If this were not so they would not be art, but merely artistic.

Can the naturalness of a successful work of art even exceed that of the thing or species in the connatural world around us? Creation is still in progress, and in its development we have our place, as have our natural relations. There is no reason, then, why the human contribution to natural history, as it is most advanced in art, should not come nearer the goal than some things in the connatural world around us. The non-human world is not idyllic, and it is our task to brighten the light we see, to the best of our ability.

This follows Friedrich Schiller's philosophy of history. The goal of culture is to find its way back to freedom in nature through reason. This double movement, forwards to meet nature while at the same time returning to it, means that the future finding of nature is preceded by loss, so that we stand on the second of three steps, harmony, decay and reunification with nature. Heinrich von Kleist compared these three steps to the transition in life from child to adult in his *Essay on Puppet Theatre*, with the matchless and memorable parable of the youth who imitated a Greek statue:

'About three years ago, I was bathing in the company of a young man whose form at that time possessed a wonderful grace. He would have been about sixteen years old then, and the first traces of vanity called up by the favour of women were just perceptible. It so happened that a short time previously we had seen the statue of the youth taking a splinter out of his foot in Paris; ... a glance thrown into the large mirror, after placing his foot on the stool to dry it, reminded him of it; he smiled and told me of his discovery. At the very same moment I had had the same impression, but whether in order to test his confidence in his grace, or to combat his vanity in a beneficial way, I laughed and retorted that he was imagining things. He flushed and raised his foot a second time to demonstrate. He failed in the attempt, however, though the action should have been easily accomplished. He raised his foot a third and a fourth time in confusion, and probably ten times in all, but in vain. He simply could not repeat the movement – What did I say to this? The

movements which he made had about them such a comic
element that I had trouble holding back my laughter. From that
day, or even from that very moment, an unimaginable change
came over the young man's behaviour. He began to stand in
front of the mirror all day long; and one after another of his
charms left him.'[32]

Kleist saw the overcoming of the crisis as being like, 'the
image in a concave mirror, which after it has moved a long
distance away, suddenly appears before us. Grace is found
again when our knowledge has travelled through eternity.' For
this reason we should 'eat once more from the tree of knowledge,
in order to return to the state of innocence', which would form
the last chapter of world history.[33] This return to innocence is
to be understood in the parable in the same way as the biblical
'becoming like children', to proceed and yet return to what has
previously existed, so that life becomes rounded.

Schiller's philosophy of history, in a very concise formulation, was that animal and flower, tree and stone 'are what we
were, and are what we are supposed to become again. We were
nature like they are, and our culture should bring us back to
nature, through reason and freedom.'[34] Culture thus lies between lost nature and the nature which is to be rediscovered,
and – the key concept – it is the bridge between the two.
Rediscovery of nature can be missed, and we are in danger of
allowing this to happen. The central part of history, which
actually is *the* natural history of humanity, will then move to
the abyss, hurried towards it by what counts as progress in the
industrial economy. This does not mean that the loss of nature
was in itself a disaster, as long as we remember to mourn lost
nature in every change and even in artistic renewal. From this
grief grows the strength to pursue the path towards becoming
anew what we once were.

In this interpretation of history, the task of art in humanity's quest for the nature we have lost, is to protect the goal,
nature which is again to be found. Schiller used this argument
for poetry, but it is equally valid for art, particularly for artistic
treatment of space. 'As nature gradually began to disappear
from human life as *experience*, and as *subject* (of action and

sensation) it rose in the poetic world as *idea* and *object* ... Poets are overall guardians of nature ... They will either *be* nature, or they will *seek* that which has been lost.'[35]

Using these alternatives Schiller distinguished between the naive and the sentimental in poetry, and also attempted to relate his work to Goethe's in this way. Two hundred years later I hold the search for lost nature to be the vital task of art, in the same way as the search for lost truth is the task of philosophy. While it is not possible to *find* them both, the goal can be present in moving towards it. The artist 'lives a little nearer to the heart of creation than is usual. And not near enough by a long way', as is inscribed on Paul Klee's gravestone.

For the future before us which we must seek, we have a beautiful image – roundness. The pre-Socratic philosopher Parmenides described being as '...like the bulk of a well rounded ball, equal in every way from the middle. For it must not be any greater or smaller here or there'.[36] This image runs through the course of history. Vincent van Gogh declared, 'Life is probably round', and, in Rilke's poem 'Anxiety' in his *Book of Pictures* we find 'And yet the round birdcall, in this moment which engenders it, rests wide as the sky above the faded forest.' 'The round being spreads its roundness,' added Bachelard, 'and radiates the peace of all things round.' ... 'It is now up to us to make the correct use of this, and to learn from it how being composes itself around the middle point.'[37]

We are so far from this roundness because human life, individual, personal, economic and political, does not revolve around the centre of existence as it ought. Even if we, as 'artists of life', look for art in life and for lost nature in art, we are still – *simul justus et peccator* – at a crossroads where everything hangs on right or wrong choice. With lost nature on one side and that to be found on the other, the aim is not immediate arrival at our goal, but rather not neglecting to take whatever steps we can towards that goal. This movement is the way to be at the goal, even today. Roundness can shine forth even in conflict, promising us the goal and giving hope; it happens when a particular day is seen as rounded, or because something is well completed. We must be mistrustful of ways which are all too

straight, which offer progress without curves; for only what is
round is enduring.

Notes

1 Schweitzer 1923/1974, II, 377

[2] Timaeus 47b

[3] 1 Cor. 15, 10

[4] 1 Cor. 3, 9

[5] Col. 1, 16

[6] *Grundlegung zur Metaphysik der Sitten*, A4

[7] ibid., A52

[8] Heraclitus, Diels-Kranz B112

[9] *Politics* 1253a3

[10] 1799, Notes in the margin of Schlegel's *Ideas*, §51

[11] A. Meyer-Abich, 1934, 1935

[12] A. Meyer-Abich 1950, 52ff

[13] A. Meyer-Abich 1935, 27

[14] *Das Allgemeine Brouillon,* §60

[15] *Politics* 1254a36f

[16] Goethe, *Werke* XIII, 316

[17] Goethe, *Werke* XIII, 45

[18] Bonhoeffer 1963, 168

[19] Liedke 1979, 144

[20] Bonhoeffer 1963, 112f

[21] Adorno, 1970, 104

[22] Sahagún 1982, 73

[23] Stifter 1857

[24] V.von Weizsäcker 1926/1987, vol.5, 35ff

[25] 23rd October, 1828

[26] Quoted by Schipperge 1984/5, 49

[27] K. W. Kapp

[28] Diels-Kranz B62

[29] ibid. B1

[30] Stone 1972

[31] *Aeneid* I, 462

[32] Kleist 1810

[33] ibid.
[34] NA vol. XX, 414
[35] NA vol. XX, 431, 26-9; 432, 22ff and 27f
[36] Diels-Kranz B8, 43-5
[37] Bachelard 1964, 214 and 209

Chapter 5

Social State and Nature State

The offer of autonomous security is a fundamental attraction of the anthropocentric view of the world and of humanity for those who no longer find it in religion. The promise of such security is the real strength of this world view. Humanity finally stands at the centre, self-validated, the measure of all things, the autonomous subject of history. It is not easy to dispel the fascination of this proud thought. Behind it, there hides the essential emotionality of the Enlightenment, yet incomplete and unenlightened. Would it not diminish us to see the measure of our actions in nature, once more at a higher level than our own? And is it not even a form of self-critical modesty not to aspire to a higher measure than ourselves in our actions? Pretensions of that sort have brought humanity enough misfortune in the past, so let us in all modesty remain our own measure!

The anthropocentric view of the world and of humanity is so fascinating, because it is so agreeable. To be both wise *and* modest – who could wish for more? Even human selfishness and lack of consideration for the rest of the world can be glossed over in the most fantastic way. Certainly it is unworthy of humanity to do everything out of mere selfishness; hence for our own sakes, we should not do everything for our own sakes. But when something is as it is just *for our sakes,* is this not confirmation of the anthropocentric approach? Aesthetic justification is a variant of this appealing fiction. According to the evidence of the previous chapter, the consequence the physiocentric view of the world and of humanity has for our actions is that culture is our debt to the world. But is culture not a human requirement, which would mean that the physiocentric approach is already contained within the anthropocentric one?

Another variant, used to evade the implications of the physiocentric way of thought, occurs when physiocentrism is interpreted as the exact opposite of anthropocentrism. Since industrial society takes account only of humanity and not at all of the connatural world, the alternative is for human interests to be subjugated as thoroughly as those of the connatural world have been. This leads to the conclusion that we should leave the world as far as possible as if we had never been here, whereas physiocentrism correctly understood recognizes the interests of both humanity and the connatural world, and balances them in such a way that culture comes into the world.

Objections of this kind, or intellectual games like aesthetic anthropocentrism, indicate quite clearly that a holistic philosophy of nature must be thought through further; and I shall be grateful for reactions to this book along these lines. Such objections are also based on assumptions which comply emotionally with the anthropocentric view of the world and of humanity, and it 'is a law with the devil and with ghosts. Where they slip inside they must come out again.'[1] A typical example is the hubris which is involved in attempting to re-establish the security lost with the loss of religion. The most succinct formulation of this hubris, to my mind, is in a declaration of the Second Vatican Council to the Roman Catholic church. It states 'that man ... is the only creature on earth created by God for its own sake'.[2] Once more devils show themselves within the church's own domain.

This statement is representative of a particular tradition in Christian theology. Taking it literally, it claims we are in the world for our own sake. That this should moreover have been God's will gives the claim a consecrated air, as a welcome bonus for those who would not have accepted the contrary from theology, but it does not set any limits. It is not openly stated that all other creatures were created for us, but this is the implication of the statement. If they had been created primarily to glorify their creator, this would probably have applied to us as well, and humanity would never have been elevated to the special position claimed for it here. Hence the statement means: We are here for our own sake, and the rest of the world is also here for our sake. It is this claim which constitutes the anthropocentric view of the world and of humanity. Politically this is manifested in the present world situation, in the assumption that the rampant economic growth of industrialized countries should be reckoned as progress par excellence, and as the only sound example to the countries of the Third World, the 'developing countries'.

Academic philosophy tends to occupy itself with the concept of will, rather than with the will itself; so it is understandable that it likes to play with ideas, such as the analysis of the requirement for culture and beauty as in itself a kind of human selfishness, mixing anthropomorphism and anthropocentrism. However, this analysis is only an academic gloss on the actual thrust of the will which has historically been such a powerful force in the anthropocentric world view. It is this will itself which must be combated in a revolution for nature. It has its roots in the Enlightenment of the eighteenth century and actually desires:

   – autonomy, not freedom, for humanity, without taking the natural world into account except for reasons of human selfishness; and in particular,

   – the autonomy of a market economy, as envisaged by the bourgeois revolution.

Both types of autonomy imply autonomy for scientific research.

The distinction between autonomy and freedom is that freedom is subject to reason and cannot exist without responsibility, whereas for autonomy absolutism is sufficient. The containment of the will to autonomy was the basic objective in the development of the modern legal state since the bourgeois revolution, through order based on freedom and reason, and it continues today to be disregarded in the behaviour of industrialized countries towards the Third World. Its evolution is punctuated by two major crises, the social crisis of the nineteenth century and the present environmental crisis. In both crises I see a chance to complete the eighteenth century Enlightenment, intellectually and politically, in a way that would finally deserve the term 'Enlightenment'. The political and philosophical opportunities for overcoming the present crisis in this fashion are the theme of this chapter.

From Social Crisis to Environmental Crisis

Insofar as solutions were found to the problem of exploitation in early capitalist society, they took the general form that every economic activity be politically restricted by social responsibility. This condition is expressed in Article 20 of the German constitution, in the statement that the country is a 'social state'. It is unusual that a particular duty of the state, in this case ensuring that the economy does not offend against the weak or against human value, should be so important politically that the whole state is named after it. Other duties, which originally had no connection with care for the poor and weak, have subsequently been moulded in that direction by the goal of the social state. The corollary is that the social state not only excludes unsocial behaviour towards a particular group of people, but upholds social justice within the whole, right across society, not only in the narrow sense of provision for the very needy. 'The social state is ... a state of social integration.'[3]

To distinguish a specific duty so that it determines the whole in a particular way makes good political sense, although it causes difficulties in the interpretation of a nation's laws. The exploitation of the poor and weak in nineteenth century industrial states indicated a lack of awareness of the whole in the division of the parts, apparent as a weakness of the general interest when set against that of individuals. One might say industrial society had got cold feet – not only feet, either, for the whole system was affected. For this reason the integrating strength of the state must be tested from the outermost point, if it is to prove its worth. This was the basic social question of the nineteenth century.

Since the foundation of the social state other problems have become more pressing than these. In the twentieth century the destruction of the environment is so pre-eminently threatening that upon it depends not only the acceptability and life-span of a particular economic system, or the fate of a particular country, but the fate of the industrial state and the survival of industrial society as a whole. The problem is analogous to the social question of the last century. Once more the forces of economic production are breaking the only frame within which they can continue to be productive. Once more individual interests are thriving at the expense of the whole, so that the social costs are greater than the costs to individuals, and business is managed at a cost to the whole. Nowadays, however, all individuals, bosses, employees, producers and consumers alike, gain some personal advantage, though to varying extents. Yet the result does not correspond to the general will. Everyone is interested only in his or her own prosperity. There is no general will to destroy the conditions that support general prosperity, to everybody's cost. Accordingly, it is once more up to the state to spell out the 'general interest' and to do so in everybody's interest.

Again, it is partly a question of protecting people particularly affected by environmental devastation from those others who particularly profit by it. Of course, it is already one of the duties of the social state to prevent discrimination, in the interest of common justice. The destruction of environmental conditions incidentally brings benefits to some at a cost to others, but it mainly affects the public as a whole in its relations with the rest of the natural world. The social state has no jurisdiction here. The whole of which the general interest must be preserved now includes not only human society, but also the world around us: animals, plants, landscapes, the water balance, and the climate. In nature, humanity is not a closed society. The question now is whether the non-human parts of nature should be regarded as part of the general public for which the state is responsible, and whether the state should accept responsibility towards them as it did towards exploited sections of society in the nineteenth century. Should the whole of which the interests are to be preserved in future be more broadly based than before, and should the state for this reason be redefined as a 'nature-state'? The idea that we should 'place the principle of protecting nature for its own sake' as 'the principle of the nature-state' alongside the principle of the social state, is one which comes from Hans-Jochen Vogel.[4] I have adopted it to put the value system of a holistic ethic into concrete constitutional terms, so that peace with nature can be made comprehensible.

It is only when public awareness has developed sufficiently that constitutional consequences can be expected to follow from the philosophical concept of the intrinsic dignity of the natural world. But since the Second Vatican Council referred to above, some things have already altered as a result of the environmental movement. The concept of the connatural world (*natürliche Mitwelt*) has achieved wide currency in society in the few years since the first appearance of my *Ways to Peace with Nature*. And the Christian churches in Germany, after a slightly restrained start in 1985, have now definitively declared that the human being may not in nature 'attend only to personal interests, but must also consider the possible effects of actions on the life-chances of other species. Everything created in fellowship with humanity has intrinsic value, independent of its utility value, because of its connection with God the Creator, sharing in His life and created for His praise ... the Protestant and Catholic churches accordingly declare that environmental protection should be formulated as an aim of the Constitution, not simply to protect the human environment, but in terms of responsibility for all creation, of protecting the natural conditions for life, and of the safeguarding nature and the environment. The Churches wish to repeat and emphasize their consensus here. Any formulation of constitutional goals which does not take the intrinsic value of non-human life into account could be used in the future as a pretext to legitimize activities which were regarded as essential to the rights and interests of humanity, although they threatened the biodiversity of the created world which is necessary for life. ... In every political decision affecting the environment human interests must be weighed against the intrinsic value of non-human life. This kind of assessment must become a political duty'[5]

Meanwhile the political parties are also moving in this direction to some extent. On the other hand, the German Supreme Administrative Court and the majority of state councillors adhere to the anthropocentric ethic, although they are not bound to do so by the constitution. The inviolability of human dignity (Article 1) is to be understood as meaning that the state should be there for people. It is intended to deny that people exist for the state, but it does not imply that the state cannot also exist for other life-forms and things, that is for the connatural world.[6] The addition suggested by the German Protestant Church, 'In its responsibility for creation the state protects the natural environment', could immediately be included in the constitution without any difficulty.

Making protection of the natural world a constitutional goal would be the signal for curbing our rampant economy in its promotion of industrial interests at the expense of the rest of the world and nature as a whole. But taking account of the intrinsic value of the natural world is so diametrically opposed to the economic interests which have dominated up till now that an additional clause, containing a further constitutional aim of the state, is not nearly sufficient to limit present practice. The basic rationale of the economy has been that the things and species of nature have *no* intrinsic value, but may have a value to us, or to some of us, as resources. That is why the protection of the connatural world must lead to a completely new validation for the state as a whole, following the example of the social state. As things are, the problem is again not only at the base, but right through the system.

What does it mean to define the industrial state not only as a social state, functioning through social integration, but beyond this, committed to the integration of industrial society into the interdependency of the natural world, as a state within nature, in that sense a 'nature-state'? Being by nature political animals, we are prepared, by the nature of the whole which is not ours alone, to form a new interdependency in nature, the political, so fulfilling our historical role. Our state should be organized so that nature as a whole can develop itself with us. If it is generally true that we bring culture into the world, the nature-state is a question of political culture. If one looks back to the 'natural state' described by Hobbes and Locke, it is clear that the bourgeois state is at heart a state of property. Locke even saw the protection of property as the real purpose of the state. Without the principle of property we could never have entered the bourgeois state. With it, however, we can no longer stay within this state. It is just the appropriation of the connatural world through the industrial process that is endangering and destroying it.

Self-Realization through Property

In bourgeois society, property is the basic principle of social and political order. Charles Darwin even thought that the drive to own property is innate, after he had watched an ape in the zoo appropriate a stone it was using as a nutcracker for its own sole use.[7] If this is so, our mission in natural history could well be to overcome property-based behaviour. My own impression is that in nature there is no property in the bourgeois sense of unrestricted availability regardless of need. But in the bourgeois order, property is the 'most widely-embracing sovereign right which the law can apply'.[8] Relationships are formed or strengthened through property, social relationships – some have stones, others do not – and relationships with the connatural world.

The bourgeois concept of property, which most people today take for granted, arose in the seventeenth and eighteenth centuries. The concept of absolute proprietorship for everybody was then a new one. 'The first man who had the idea of enclosing a piece of ground and maintaining, "This belongs to me", and who found others naive enough to believe him, was the true founder of bourgeois society,' declared Rousseau at the start of the second part of his *Treatise on the Causes of Inequality*. One must not take for granted that people will make such claims to one another, or in connection with nature. Legal history demonstrates many ways of exercising power over things and species. Before the French Revolution, in particular, there was feudal tenure and common property, where responsibility was distributed and weighed on a hierarchical basis. By contrast, the bourgeois concept of property is so constituted that the political absolutism of the eighteenth century seems to have reappeared in a property absolutism of the citizen after the French Revolution. Since then, the whole of our society has become bourgeois, and we have a kind of absolutism for everybody.

In terms of religious history, the rise of the bourgeois claim to property derives from the process of individualization in the modern era. On the other hand, in the books of the bible, in spite of geographical neighbours who thought differently, no one is himself the owner of anything at all in the world, for: 'The earth is the Lord's and all that is in it, the world, and those who live in it.'[9] God is '*the* owner ... first of people and their land, then also of individuals and their property, and finally, as creator, of the whole world'.[10] Our relations with things are embedded into personal relations with their creator and sole owner. It is in this light that we must view the eighth commandment, Thou shalt not steal. In the German constitution[11] the guarantee to property is aimed at protecting the individual's right to control his or her own economic life from state interference. 'Property is protected in constitutional terms, because it safeguards the freedom of the individual, as the real basis of personal existence and development.'[12] This teleological interpretation, derived from the aim, follows the precedent set by the Federal Constitutional Court in its judgment that the fundamental right to property exists in order that the individual 'should be enabled to take responsibility for the course of his own life'.[13] This clarification of the right to property was based on a judgment of the Federal Supreme Court in 1952: 'The individual incorporated in a state requires an area of ownership which is strictly protected in legal terms, for the sake of his freedom and dignity, in order that he may live freely, responsible for himself, and will not become a mere object, overwhelmed by too powerful state forces.'[14]

The economic independence and freedom from state interference guaranteed by owning property corresponded to the
interests of the bourgeoisie in the French Revolution. Ownership of actual goods was what was meant. Independence through
private property only ever happened to a small part of the
population, but it was adopted as a paradigm for the developing
aims of capitalism. Property was seen as 'the extension of the
individual's physical being',[15] as 'the stuff of revelation within
human individuality',[16] or as the 'bastion' of personality.[17] An
empty sack cannot stand upright, as Benjamin Franklin once
said.

Self-realization through property! This goal of the bourgeois epoch has been propounded emphatically even by political
theorists from otherwise quite opposing factions. Unmodified,
it no longer makes sense for us in a democratic social state, if we
bear in mind the consequences of the bourgeois claim to property which have now become evident in nature and society. Yet
it is still a commonplace that property brings status. If we are
to pave a way for different claims in future, we must be clear
about the motives behind developments so far, as they are still
flourishing today. They lie in the relationship between the
individual and the state, which is the mainspring of liberalism,
and in the relationship of the industrial economy with nature,
which surprisingly has been best expressed by Hegel.

According to bourgeois ideology, it would be pleasantest to
live without any form of state organization. This is only possible
in the ideal natural circumstances described by Locke, where
everyone can appropriate whatever he wants and is capable of
getting from the natural world without impinging on others.
Sadly, this stage passed with increasing population density,
and in any case the invention of money meant people could own
more land than they could actually work themselves. This led
to interference of individuals with the property of others, and
'men unite into societies, that they may have the united strength
of the whole society to secure and defend their properties'[18] In
this analysis the state is only necessary to protect property,
from the interference of other people or other nations. There
would otherwise be no need for the state at all. Accordingly all

power of government is 'entrusted with this condition, and for this end, that men might have and secure their properties.'[19] and political power is 'a right of making laws ... for the regulation and preservation of property.'[20] The 'chief end'[21] which makes individual citizens combine in bourgeois society is the protection of their property.

The bourgeois idea that the state was there fundamentally to protect property was stretched to the limit historically when some people had no property, and had to sell their labour to utilize the property of others as a means of production. The capitalist claim to property brought a rising industrial society to the very edge of its capabilities for the first time through exploitation of the labour of the have-nots. The development towards a social state has at least solved the social question, since it is no longer necessary to own property in order to ensure one's existence. One could say, in Gehlen's words, that 'today mere membership of the state is enough to ensure the means of life'.[22] A citizen in an industrial society lives off wages, a salary, a pension or in certain cases from welfare benefits, not from property income as the idea was originally conceived.

This development can be described as a change in the understanding of property. The social state extends freedom in ways other than those envisaged in liberalism, but equally achieves functional property ownership, in the sense of protecting the right to property.[23] In legal terms this extension of the concept of property has actually taken place in reality, as a result of a judgment of the German Supreme Court in 1924,[24] indicating that people's annuities would also be covered by the protection of property. However, by such teleological interpretation we come to a point where ultimately all property does is make economic self-determination possible. This resumes Locke's original philosophical conception of property, though politically his idea has been narrowed down to material property. Would it not rather have been better to give up the bourgeois principle of property ownership after its historical flourishing, rather than sublimating it as if there could be no freedom without property?

After all, the commercial enterprises which were once

proof of the idea that the function of property was to protect freedom are hardly recognizable in their present form. The separation of ownership from possession has fundamentally changed the situation. A good example is the failure of Dürig's heroic attempt to align the guaranteed basic rights of corporations[25] with the basic rights of individual persons. 'The corporation as a legal person cannot satisfactorily be described in terms of room for its owners' material development. It is not a bastion of their personalities.'[26]

In the social state and in the development of the administration of justice there has actually been a move away from the early liberal concept of property, although this concept has not been given up. In Article 14 of the German Constitution, property, with a social commitment as at present, is guaranteed. We shall leave aside the question of how far this commitment goes when, as in Germany, 1.7% of the population controls 70% of the country's production. In any case, the constitution of the social state is the success brought by a first step away from the original bourgeois concept of property. In my opinion this first step must be followed by a second one, for, by endangering the basis of life, the claim to property has brought industrial society to the very edge of its capabilities once again.

The first crisis, which was social, arose from the relationships in society which had been brought about or strengthened as a result of property ownership. The second crisis, the environmental one, has arisen out of the pretence of owning the connatural world. The problem of uneven distribution of property was at least seen from the beginning as a curtailment of the freedom of fellow human beings; but nature, so far, has hardly featured in the development of the understanding of property. That any account at all should be taken of it was denied in a particularly extreme way by Hegel, a denial which was entirely characteristic of industrial society's further development.

For Hegel the mind is the sphere of being and freedom, while nature is the realm of having and bondage. This goes so far that 'I...*am* alive, and *have* an organic body'.[27] Man only lives *in* his body in the same way as a helmsman lives in his ship at sea, but he is not physical or a part of nature; man is only spiritual. Even his own body is external to him, as is the rest of the material world. According to Hegel, a person, the mind individualized in a single human, needs all the same 'an outer sphere for its freedom'.[28] This sphere is property, 'in' which to exist as if in an extended body. 'Only with property does the Person achieve reason',[29] although this property itself is 'an *object*, without freedom, personality *or rights*'.[30] 'Each person thus has the right to displace an object and make it his own, for the thing as an externality has no purpose of its own ... Living things (animals) are also externalities, and as such are themselves objects ... To appropriate something means to manifest my supremacy over objects ... I give to the living thing a different soul from the one it had, when it becomes my property – I give it my own'.[31] Thus we have 'an absolute right to appropriate any object',[32] whether living or not. Not only are these things without rights: we are also permitted to erase their souls and replace them with our own bourgeois specimen, as we transform them into property.

The capacity for abstract thought permits humanity to escape intellectually from nature, and to understand nature as pure externality – in Hegel's words as 'the external itself'.[33] This is a reiteration of the Cartesian division of the world into thought (*res cogitans*) and that which is extended in space (*res extensa*). Descartes' natural philosophy, with its classification of animals as mere machines, already contains in its essence the assumption which Hegel proclaims as normative for human activity in nature. Oddly enough, industrial society has never used Hegel to justify the brutality with which everything not human is completely bereft of rights and even of its own soul by the towering human will. As a philosopher for industrial society Hegel should gain more recognition than he is generally given. What he designated as an 'object' is known today as a resource, and we understand and treat the world of nature as a resource in the very way recommended by him.

Hegel's *Natural Law*, the paradoxical subtitle for his *Philosophy of Law* which maintains that nature is without rights, was instrumental in the legal interpretation of nature in the nineteenth century, especially in the German Civil Code

(1897). There it is stated: 'The owner of an object may do as he wishes with it, provided he does not come into conflict with the law, or infringe upon the rights of other persons, and may exclude all others from effecting it.'[34] The first draft of 1888 even stated that the owner could deal with his own 'arbitrarily'. In fact the law cramps the supremacy so assigned to the bourgeois will with a wealth of restrictions and exclusions. Nevertheless, in the Civil Code in general, and in modern law almost exclusively, these lead only to the presumption that in dealing with objects as one wishes neither other human beings nor humanity at large may be put at a disadvantage. As far as the 'object' goes, there is no restriction on doing what one likes. 'Objects' in the legal sense are generally 'material objects'; things and living organisms, even parts of the human body are included, but not the whole human being.

One could object that by definition the Civil Code cannot do anything other than simply regulate human relationships. But the Criminal Code deals with 'objects' in the same sense as the Civil Code, and under Public Law nature fares no better. For example, the understanding of natural things as 'objects' is clear from the wording of the law protecting against harmful emissions. 'Animals, plants and other objects' are to be protected from harmful environmental effects.[35] Whether something is animate or inanimate, it will be treated as an object. The Protection of Animals Act (1972) deviates from this. It is intended to protect animals for their own sakes, but this intention is seldom invoked in the application of the law. According to the traditional legal understanding of nature, things and living creatures must be considered only as far as humans are affected, not because of any intrinsic value they have in nature's whole. This kind of appropriation of our connatural world has been regarded all along as a way to human freedom, but from the beginning it was based on oppression, both of other human beings and of the connatural world. Neither kind of oppression is justifiable today. The Enlightenment of the eighteenth century overcame the absolutism of kings, and in its completion it must now put an end to the absolutism of everybody.

Criticism of the bourgeois rape of nature began early. Novalis wrote that 'Nature does not want to be the exclusive possession of a single man. As property it becomes transformed into a dangerous poison which drives peace away, and the corrupting urge for the possessor to draw everything into his circle is linked with unending worries and wild passions. Thus the ground is undermined beneath its owner, and soon he is buried in a yawning abyss'.[36] A century later Otto von Gierke described it as 'a barbaric absurdity ... that a part of our planet can belong to a single man in the same way as an umbrella or a banknote'.[37] And Marx declared in the third volume of *Das Kapital* 'From the point of view of an advanced economy and society, the private ownership of the earth by individuals will appear as fatuous as the private ownership of humans by humans. A whole society, a nation, or even all societies taken together, do not possess the earth. They are only its tenants, its beneficiaries, and as *boni patres familias* must leave it, in an improved state, to future generations'.[38] Of course people should be able to feel at home somewhere, but to achieve this is it really necessary to own a piece of land?

The distance between the social accountability for property and an analogous natural commitment is not as great as it at first appears. This is because the capitalist absolutism of property treats the human and the connatural world equally as resources for material gain, and the denial of workers' rights was scarcely less than the denial of rights to the connatural world. Their souls too were sacrificed to the overweening desire for property. In one instance it was the workers who suffered, in the other the connatural world, but the exploitation was identical in both cases.

An apposite essay by Hans-Jochen Vogel[39] illustrates how the forms of argument used in the criticism of social exploitation can be directly transferred to nature. Vogel describes how the social crisis of capitalism, in the 'precedence of individual over general interests', led to a fundamental modification of the bourgeois concept of property. Subsequently 'property became embedded in a comprehensive order ... in which citizens as well as the state had a responsibility for the common good'.[40] In the social state, which is not just a welfare state but much more a state of social integration, property takes its place in a social context. If this sensible step were taken in the environmental crisis, the argument for this extension would be that the liberal concept of property gave the interests of the individual precedence over those of the community, and *gave human interests precedence over those of nature as a whole.* Hence, it is now essential to recognize that property is embedded in a whole world order, with citizens as well as the state bearing responsibility for the common good and *for the connatural world within nature's whole.* Property then implies an obligation not only to society but *to nature. There is a commitment to nature corresponding to the commitment to society.* This does not mean that extensive property should be restricted externally, for political reasons, but that on the contrary the definition and scope of what individual property *can* be derives from the whole. The natural and social orders together create the framework for dealing with things and living creatures as property, as far as property is permissible at all.

The legal argument for the social accountability of property in the Constitution can be transferred to a similar natural commitment. It runs: 'The human person as portrayed in the Constitution is, in the words of the German Federal Constitutional Court, not an autonomous individual, but a member of a community with many responsibilities towards it. This view of the relationship between the individual and the community must be reflected in any thinking about property.'[41] All that would be needed here is to add that not only is the individual part of a human community, of which membership is essential to his or her humanity, but that this is equally true for humanity as a part of nature. The intention is to refer property to an order that makes individuals responsible for both fellow humans and for nature, so as to legitimate its use in the framework of this holistic order. The argument then runs: the human being is no longer considered to be an autonomous individual, but rather someone who is a member of a human community and of *the community of nature*, with many responsibilities towards *both* of these. Whether in nature or in society, property must not be used autonomously, but only committed to this dual whole.

Commitments of Ownership, and the Dignity of Nature – Considerations for a Future German Constitution

What would the consequences be for a future German constitution, if the country were both a social state and a nature state? I think such a constitution should be developed from that of the former West Germany, but it should not be the same, since the west too has much to learn. If the mistakes made in the east up to now are avoided in future, the western sector should make an equal effort to avoid its own mistakes, so that both parts of the country can leave both sets of errors behind at the same time. The common political constitution is the best place to express what has been learnt on both sides, and to make the public aware of it by a plebiscite.

The 1949 Constitution did not regard human beings as a part of nature, bound to perceive personal interests which concern the connatural world in terms of a responsibility to nature as a whole. Two great and important steps are required to extend the circle of responsibility which should be the only permissible context for property in future. We have seen from the considerations of this chapter so far that one step has already been made. The second, which remains to be taken, means moving beyond the first, but in fundamentally the same direction. The first step was initiated long ago, in the agenda of the French Revolution, for in the French constitution of 1791 it is stated – as in Kant – that freedom means being able to do anything that does not harm another person. We are still very far even from satisfying the requirement that fellow human beings at least should not be harmed through the exercise of individual freedom. The aim should be to deal with the rest of the world in such a way that other people, including people in the Third World and future generations, should not have to suffer from disturbance to, pollution of, or any other destruction of their environment. This aim could easily be incorporated in the constitution, by the expression of a basic human right with regard to nature, a proposition which has been discussed on several occasions.[42] The reason it has not been adopted is that it could lead a scarcely imaginable flood of legal cases, because the circle of those acknowledged to be affected by environmental damage and so, in principle, having just cause for complaint, would be vastly increased by the extension to all citizens of the basic right to live in a healthy environment. If the state were forced to justify its insufficient exercise of duty towards the environment, it would benefit both the vitality of our democracy and the protection of the environment required for life. However, I am not in favour of such a basic right, since the anthropocentric world view, that nature is to be possessed rather than lived, reaches its peak here, and the property-based absolutism of everybody would be unimpeded. I believe that peace with nature should be found in a legal community, following the paradigm of the modern legal state, but rights must not be restricted to humanity.

To define our state further as a nature state does not conflict with the sense of the Constitution or its development so far. In its early liberal interpretation the constitution in fact only regulated the relationship between citizens and the state, in accordance with the aims of the French revolution. In particular, private property and the basic rights of individuals were to be protected from interference by the state. However, the exploitation of some citizens by others has anyway shown it could not remain at this stage without further addition. It was a step beyond the original sense of the constitution to take in the goals of the social state, in the interests of social integration. In the meantime the basic rights to defence against state interference developed, providing on the one hand positive directions for citizens' behaviour, and on the other claims which could be made on the state. For example, the responsibility to use information in the public interest to the best of one's knowledge and in good conscience pertains to the freedom of the press, and freedom of employment is linked in a democracy to the expectation that one should be able to receive education which provides training for the desired job. From such development arises a claim on the constitution that it should support peace and consensus within community life.

If property is now to be embedded in a social and natural order, and thus legitimated, so that citizens and the state have a responsibility not just for the common good, but also for the connatural world within nature's whole, the 'nature-state' should take its place alongside the social state as a constitutional goal. Refining the constitution so that it supports peace with nature as well as social peace has become a necessary consequence of development in the light of the environmental crisis.

Since our relationship with the connatural world and with nature's whole has never yet been a theme in the history of the constitution, incremental changes will not be enough. This means that nature's role must be examined in principle and right from the beginning, not just in the clauses relating to the social state, such as Articles 20 and 28 of the German Constitution, which I cited previously. Even the social state probably still needs a similar firm position in the constitution. It must be made clear that for both social and nature states, a new level of constitutional development is reached. In view of the environmental destruction brought about through the appropriation of the connatural world by industrial society, the constitution should give us a lead straight away in its preamble, not only for our awareness of 'our responsibility before God and man' but *for our responsibility towards nature* as well.

Human Dignity

The present system of basic rights, the foundation of our modern constitution, was built up on the base of human dignity. If the ground of our existence in the world is now seen as fellowship not only with other humans but with the connatural world as well, there are consequences for the future understanding of human dignity and its vulnerability. The original interpretation of the constitution is that the state is there for man and not man for the state. An injury done to one person's human dignity by another must now be seen as an injury to the other's dignity as well. But there is as yet no consensus that the way we treat animals and plants is also a question of human dignity. The necessary transformation would be best served in my view by recognizing in the constitution and in individual laws the dignity of the connatural world, particularly of the higher animals, the earth and the seas, of life itself, and of nature as a whole. It seems that talking about the dignity of the sea and so forth is in a high degree anthropomorphic, but this is inevitable with human language, and the use of the word 'dignity' is probably the most appropriate to remind us of the respect we have forgotten.

As proposed in *Ways to Peace with Nature,* a statement such as the following might additionally be included: 'Humanity evolved in the course of natural history, together with animals and plants, as well as the earth, water, air and fire. Humans have the capacity to recognize and change the world, of which they are a part, in a unique way. A particular responsibility thus falls on them, for protecting the interests of nature as a whole. Humanity must relate itself to the connatural world, not only because of human interests but for its own sake, for its own dignity.'

Individual Freedom

The positive content of the next basic right, the free development of personality,[43] must also be thought through again. This is particularly so in dealing with risks, which was a matter for consideration even before the environmental crisis, but the more so today. No one should in fact be hindered from undergoing risks as an individual, as long as they do not offend against moral law, and if the consequences in any given case are borne by the risk-taker. One may ski, climb mountains, sail, smoke cigarettes, swallow swords, eat a bad diet and so forth. However, the extent to which third parties may be endangered or burdens placed on the general public is quite another question. This is particularly relevant at the moment in the case of car travel. The social costs are twice as great as the cost to private individuals, and every third death caused by traffic accidents is a 'third party', either a pedestrian or a cyclist; in towns this figure even rises to two in three. As a result of this particular free development of personality thousands of citizens are killed each year by their fellows. This is an unacceptable situation, and to permit it is in my view a grave breach of duty in the state's obligation to protect the individual. The right to life, and to protection from bodily injury, should certainly not be interpreted in this way. Posterity's view of the collective frenzy on our roads will scarcely be better than our view of the burning of witches in the late Middle Ages and the early modern era, and not only because of the larger number of people killed in traffic accidents.

The same is true with regard to the destruction of the connatural world. The development of the individual personality can only be called free if it takes place within the holistic circle of responsibility, as developed in Chapter Three. Living at the cost of the Third World, of posterity, and of the connatural world, is a development of personality which is autonomous, but it is not free, and should not be described as such.

Freedom of Speech and Scientific Freedom

Similar consequences which I can only indicate briefly here pertain to the basic right to freedom of speech.[44] The obstructions of the state which stood in the way of the mature citizen's freedom of expression are long gone, but there is a lack of readiness to exercise the duty to form free opinion which is essential to democratic industrial society. It is true that people are not all equally well equipped to form their political opinions; but even in public enquiries, citizens have shown how to argue against overbearing and biased experts.[45]

Now that democracy has proved its stability over decades, I consider it essential to include participatory elements in the German constitution. I am not thinking primarily plebiscites, but mostly of wider participation by the public in the advisory process which precedes decisions. A real lack in our democracy is that the committees which decide by majority usually have insufficient knowledge of what they are voting about. This situation could be improved by greater public participation, and even consultative referenda, as in Sweden. A more critical public awareness could only be of benefit to the political parties as well. This can only come about when citizens' opinions are taken into account in the formation of political policy to a much greater extent than has been the case.

Sadly, we are also far from understanding that the freedom of scientists can no longer be considered a 'free lunch'. A free action is distinguished from one which is lacking in freedom in that the actor cannot push his responsibility onto another 'responsible party', but carries it himself. In science and technology too, freedom means being responsible for one's own actions, not freedom from responsibility. For the scientist, this responsibility is gravest in the decision which precedes all scientific work, as to what he considers worth knowing. The public generally transfers its respect for scientific results to science itself, but the two are separate. With the arrival of results, scientific action, what the scientist calls science, is already at an end. Somehow the scientist 'knows' which questions to pursue, but this knowledge is completely different in quality from his knowledge of the results; the latter can be proved, the former not, and only these latter are what the public regards as science. One could say, somewhat paradoxically, that science is not as scientific as its results. A historical example of this is the neglect of nature in cultural studies, which I described in the previous chapter.

Freedom of Work

The problem of risk returns with the basic right of freedom of work.[46] No one should be prevented from taking personal risks in the course of work, as long as moral law is not infringed and the risk-taker is prepared to bear the damage in any given case. But in general this is not the case in our industrial economy, where many, and perhaps most jobs – independent of dangers in the workplace – involve risks to the general public. Let us assume that in a particular case there is a probability of only one in ten million per year that someone will die of the effects of the economic process. This is a relatively small risk, corresponding to the risk taken during a ten minute flight in a passenger aircraft, and to only a thousandth of the risk undergone during car travel. However, it still means eight cases of death a year in West Germany. The state would never permit eight named citizens to be killed for the economic advantage of individual producers and consumers, or even of the general public, but statistically with that probability there will certainly be on average eight deaths per year.

As a punishment for the murder of Minos' son, the Athenians had to pay a toll of seven girls and seven youths every nine years, to be fed to the Minotaur. Otherwise they would be struck by Zeus with famine and plague. Virgil reports that the youths and girls were chosen by lot, a similar sort of choice through probability. One would think that the age of such a human sacrifice is past. But how is the toll of lives in the Athenian state distinguished from the toll in ours, except that in our case the sacrifice is not made to avoid plague and famine, but merely in order to produce goods for our consumption? Is there any justification in our affluent society for the state to allow individual people to be sacrificed for economic reasons? Laws are not actually about whether Mrs. A or Mr. Z may be killed, but about whether people may be killed.

There is no need to expatiate on how freedom of work is exercised in the industrial economy at the cost of the Third World, posterity and the connatural world. The risk problem shows that with our present form of economy we are fundamentally on the wrong track, if we consider the whole structure of responsibility as set out in Chapter Three.

Property

Through the social crisis, property was redefined. But because the Enlightenment has not yet been completed, this redefinition has not prevented obsession with property from driving our society to the brink of its existence again in the environmental crisis. Drawing conclusions from this is made more difficult because an understanding of property which was on the face of it different from ours drove communist countries even more quickly over the edge than ours has done, so that the western style economy is now held up as an example to these eastern countries. In this situation I tend towards the radical conclusion that there is no such thing as property in the bourgeois sense. *Actually nothing belongs to us*. The world does not belong to us, for we belong to it; we are here as tenants with a task to fulfil.

The things that can continue to be called property when their commitment to nature and society has been fulfilled really have almost nothing to do with the original bourgeois concept of property. To interpret property in sublimated (teleological) form as the vehicle for individual responsibility, but from now on in all eight circles of responsibility, would abolish property in the bourgeois sense and hence be as senseless as renaming all public transport 'cars' after the abolition of automobiles. Property in the bourgeois sense of autonomy has no role to play here. Hegel's criticism of Plato, that the 'idea of the Platonic state' would 'do people the injustice of rendering them incapable of owning property'[47] has been proved wrong through the actions of industrial society. We are really not entitled to private property in the Hegelian sense.

We are not concerned here with mere definitions, but with the incorporation of the industrial economy into a cultural frame. This incorporation has been successful to the extent that claims to property in the eighteenth century sense are no longer recognized, while a commitment to society is embodied in our constitution. Putting claims to property in more concrete terms, with an added commitment to nature, would be politically possible and is a natural consequence of development so far.

Reaching the same goal through, for example, feudal tenure rather than through property, would be politically pointless, since industrial society's need for property seems to be closely bound up with its suppression of death. Finding security in oneself and in property is a substitute for the lost security of religion. Property is today a bastion against death, no longer one against the state.

If we continue on the path which began with committing property to a social obligation, then Article 14, Clause 2 of the German constitution, which at present reads, 'Property carries obligations. Its use should simultaneously serve the good of the general public', would have to be extended in a future constitution to bring in an obligation that property should also be used to serve the good of nature. In the previous chapters I have presented what I hope is a decisive case for doing this. This obligation to nature should have as many levels as the circles of responsibility developed earlier. This means that

> – as I should not only be at home in my flat, but also in the apartment block, the street, the suburb, the town etc. and also that I

> – and as I am not only this individual, but equally am the son of my parents, European, a human being, a living organism and a part of nature's whole.

My property as well belongs not only to me as an individual, but in a wider sense to those to whose co-existence I owe my own: my relatives, my nation, humanity, posterity, the community of living things and nature's whole. It is self-evident that with these levels of property each remove indicates a change in universality, so that property belonging to the people, for example, does not mean that my property belongs equally to other individual citizens, or that it is actually the state's property. It remains my own, but it actually commits me with reference to everything which pertains to me, to my relations, my nation, humanity, the connatural world, and to nature's whole.

Up to now the many building regulations which dictate

how buildings should blend into a town have been felt as restrictions on private choice, but the participation of property in the whole means that these restrictions are rather definitions of what may be considered property. The levels are reminiscent of the way a piece of land in the feudal system belonged to the farmer, to the knight, to the prince and to the emperor, but to each in his own way, so that there were in principle no conflicting claims.

If it is understood in these holistic terms, the obligation to nature incurred in property clearly embraces the social obligation. Insofar as my property also belongs to my people, it must serve the whole society through social integration, which is the aim of the social state. This means that I may not damage the integrity of society as a whole by my individual treatment of what belongs to me. Moving beyond the social state to the nature state, this should also hold true for the integrity of nature's whole, which includes society.

The Nature-State and the Legal Community of Nature

The holistic concept of graded property differs fundamentally from the idea of the connatural world being placed at humanity's disposal. This difference is similar to the one between the modern legal state in its inner workings and a tribal society, or between the nature-state and bourgeois absolutism everybody. However, the Civil Code is at heart a property order, and rests on the idea that the world is made up of objects, with each object either belonging or not belonging to an individual or an institution. How could the law be brought into line with an understanding of property as outlined above? In *Ways to Peace with Nature* I argued that the kind of internal peace achieved in the modern legal state gives an up-to-date model for peace with nature. It would also lead to a corresponding awareness of injustice, so that, as Christopher Stone has suggested,[48] rights could be given to animals, plants, landscapes etc., although these rights would not all be the same. I still maintain this position, but I need not develop it further here, since the comprehensive monograph by Jörg Leimbacher has subsequently appeared[49] and the discussion has moved forward in the ideas of Sitter,[50] to a linkage between the rights of the natural world and the 'state of nature'. In the meantime the concept of *Natürliche Mitwelt* – the connatural world – has become a part of legal language, beginning with a judgement of the supreme court of Hessen in 1985. In any case, although I think that at our level of political culture this approach is appropriate, legal rights for the connatural world are only one way to recognize its intrinsic value; so that criticism of such a legal approach does not necessarily affect the idea of the connatural world's dignity as conceived in this book.

The concept of a 'nature-state', a state within nature, may seem to be even stranger than the extension of human law to protect the connatural world. Most people might think of an ant colony, rather than of Kant's natural order in human history, or of nature becoming political in us in human history. But this is the idea, so that the state participates in the natural order in the same way as humanity participates in nature. It is clear that there is a blind spot in our awareness, which makes the connection between nature and state seem so displeasing. I am thinking of how the laws governing social behaviour should be in harmony with the laws of nature, but are not. The idea that nature is the realm of being and must be understood only in descriptive terms is an attempt to suppress this uneasiness.

The strangeness of the idea of a nature-state shows how the disparities which have broken out in the reality of the environmental crisis are rooted in our consciousness, so that our thinking corresponds to wrong actions. Environmental problems have actually arisen in industrial society through conflict between the natural and the legal order. The gulf between these two orders which harbours destruction *is*, literally, the environmental crisis. If nature and the law could once more be joined together, then the nature-state would emerge as an order which would acknowledge our participation in the whole through peace with nature. What this would bring is a world where nature would be regained, and freedom gained: a new state of nature. It would bring a natural situation, where thought and action rounded out together, and where the opportunity nature has in humanity would be fulfilled.

Notes

[1] Mephistopheles in Goethe's *Faust* I, 1410f
[2] Rahner/Vorgrimler 1968, 471f
[3] Vogel 1976, 23
[4] Vogel 1987
[5] *Gemeinsame Erklärung* 1989, 37f
[6] Kuhlmann 1990, 172
[7] Darwin 1871
[8] Wolff/Raiser 1957, 173
[9] Ps.24, 1
[10] Locher 1954, 18
[11] Article 14
[12] J. Meyer-Abich 1980, 58
[13] BVerfGE 24, 367/389
[14] BGHZ [GS] 6, 270/276, quoted from J. Meyer-Abich 1980
[15] Bluntschli 1886, 288
[16] Stahl 1978, 251
[17] Dahlmann 1815/1886, 36
[18] Locke 1690/1946, §136
[19] ibid. §139
[20] ibid. §3
[21] ibid. §85
[22] Gehlen 1960, 168
[23] J. Meyer-Abich 1980, 67
[24] ibid., 18ff, 59
[25] Article 19, Sect.3 in the German Constitution
[26] J. Meyer-Abich, 1980, 102
[27] *Philosophy of Law*, §47, my italics
[28] ibid., §41
[29] ibid.
[30] ibid., §42, my italics
[31] ibid., §44

[32] ibid.
[33] ibid., §42 and passim
[34] Bürgerliches Gesetzbuch, §903
[35] Bundesimmissions Schutzgesetz, §1
[36] *Heinrich von Ofterdingen*, Ch.5
[37] Gierke 1889/1948, 21
[38] Marx 1894/1973, 784
[39] Vogel 1976
[40] ibid., 20
[41] ibid., 23
[42] Steiger 1975
[43] Article 2, Grundgesetze
[44] Article 5, Grundgesetze
[45] Ueberhorst 1984, 257
[46] Article 12, Grundgesetze
[47] *Philosophy of Law* 46
[48] Leimbacher 1988
[49] Sitter 1987
[50] Stone 1972

Bibliography

Adorno, Theodor W., *Ästhetische Theorie* (Complete Works vol. VII). Frankfurt a.M. 1970

Bachelard, Gaston, *La Poétique de l'Espace*, 4th edn. Paris 1964

Birnbacher, Dieter, *Verantwortung für zukünftige Generationen*. Stuttgart 1988

Bluntschli, Johann K., *Allgemeine Staatslehre*, 6th edn. Stuttgart 1886

Bonhoeffer, Dietrich, *Ethik,* ed. Bethge von Eberhard. München 1963

Burke, Edmund, 'Speech to the electors of Bristol ...' 1774. In *Edmund Burke on Government, Politics and Society*, ed. B.W. Hill, pp. 156-8. Hassocks, Brighton, 1975

Dahlmann, Friedrich Christoph, *Ein Wort über die Verfassung* (1815), ed. C. Varrentrap. Stuttgart 1886

Darwin, Charles, *The Descent of Man, and Selection in Relation to Sex*. London 1871

Dawkins, Richard, *The Selfish Gene*, Oxford 1976

German Bundestag (ed.), *Protecting the Earth's Atmosphere: An International Challenge*. Interim Report of the Study Commission of the 11th German Bundestag 'Preventive Measures to Protect the Earth's Atmosphere'. Bonn 1989 (in English)

German Bundestag (ed.), *Protecting the Tropical Forests: A High-priority International Task*. 2nd Report of the Enquete-Commission 'Preventive Measures to Protect the Earth's Atmosphere' of the 11th German Bundestag. Bonn 1990 (in English)

Diels, Hermann, *Die Fragmente der Vorsokratiker*. Greek and German, corr. edn. ed. Walther Kranz. Berlin 1951

Diodorus Siculus, *Bibliotheca Historica*, Ed. Fr. Vogel. Vol. I. Stuttgart 1964

Dürckheim, Graf Karlfried von, 'Untersuchungen zum gelebten Raum. Erlebniswirklichkeit und ihr Verständnis. Systematische Untersuchungen II'. In *Neue Psychologische Studien.*, ed. Felix Krueger, vol.16 no.4: 'Psychologische Optik', pp. 383-480. München 1932

Eisler, *Wörterbuch der philosophischen Begruffe*. Berlin 1930

Erdheim, Mario, *Die Psychoanalyse und das Unbewußte in der Kultur. Aufsätze 1980-1987*. Frankfurt a.M. 1988

Evangelische Kirche in Deutschland (EKD), Schreiben des Bundesbevollmächtigten des Rates am Sitz der Bundesrepublik Deutschland vom 13. Okt. 1987 zur Anhörung des Rechtsausschusses zum Staatsziel >>Umweltschutz<< am 11. Okt. 1987

Frankena, W.K., 'Ethics and the environment'. In *Ethics and Problems of the 21st Century*, ed. K.E. Goodpaster and K.M. Sayre, pp. 3-30. Notre Dame/London 1979

Gehlen, Arnold, 'Soziologische Aspekte des Eigentumsproblems in der Industrie-Gesellschaft'. In *Eigentum und Eigentümer* (pub. W. Raymond-Stiftung) vol.1, pp. 164ff. Köln/Opladen 1960

Gemeinsame Erklärung, *Gott ist ein Freund des Lebens. Herausforderungen und Aufgaben beim Schutz des Lebens*. Gemeinsame Erklärung des Rates der Evangelischen Kirche in Deutschland und der Deutschen Bischofskonferenz... Gütersloh 1989

Gierke, Otto von, *Die soziale Aufgabe des Privatrechts* (1889). Frankfurt a.M. 1948

Goethe, Johann Wolfgang von, *Werke*, Hamburger Ausgabe (HA) in 14 vols., 8th ed. München 1981

Kloas, J./Kuhfeld, H., *Verkehrsverhalten im Vergleich*. Beiträge zur Strukturforschung des DIW, Heft 96, 1987

Kükelhaus, Hugo, *Unmenschliche Architektur – Von der Tierfabrik zur Lernanstalt*. Köln 1973

Kükelhaus, Hugo/Lippe, Rudolf zur, *Entfaltung der Sinne: Ein >>Erfahrungsfeld<< zur Bewegung und Besinnung*. Frankfurt a.M 1982

Kuhlmann, Hartmut, 'Aufnahme der Mitgeschöpflichkeit ins Grundgesetz?' In *Juristenzeitung* 4 (1990), pp. 162-75

Leimbacher, Jörg, *Die Rechte der Natur*. Basel/Frankfurt a. M. 1988

Liedke, Gerhard, *Im Bauch des Fisches. Ökologische Theologie*. Stuttgart/Berlin 1979

Locher, Gottfried Wilh., *Der Eigentumsbegriff als Problem evangelischer Theologie*. Zurich 1954

Locke, John, *The Second Treatise of Government* (1690), ed. J.W. Gough. Oxford, 1946

Marquard, Odo, 'Über die Unvermeidlichkeit der Geisteswissenschaften'. In *Ders.: Apologie des Zufalligen*. Stuttgart 1986

Marx, Karl, *Das Kapital* (1894). Vol. 6 (Marx-Engels-Werke XXV). Berlin 1973

Meyer-(Abich), Adolf, *Ideen und Ideale der biologischen Erkenntnis – Beitrage zur Theorie und Geschichte der biologischen Ideologien*. Leipzig 1934

Meyer(-Abich), Adolf, *Krisenepochen und Wendepunkte des biologischen Denkens*. Jena 1935

Meyer-Abich, Adolf, 'Zur Logik der Unbestimmtheitsbeziehungen'. In *Die Ganzheit in Philosophie und Wissenschaft - Othmar Spann zum 70*, ed. W. Heinrich, pp. 47-76. Wien 1950

Meyer-Abich, Jann, 'Der Schutzzweck der Eigentumsgarantie - Leistung, Freiheit, Gewaltenteilung. Zur teleologischen Auslegung des Art'. 14 Abs. 1 GG (Schriften zum Öffentlichen Recht Bd. 384). Berlin 1980

Meyer-Abich, Klaus Michael, *Wege zum Frieden mit der Natur – Praktische Naturphilosophie für die Umweltpolitik* (Ways to Peace with Nature). München 1984

Meyer-Abich, Klaus Michael, *Wissenschaft für die Zukunft – Holistisches Denken in ökologischer und gesellschaftlicher Verantwortung*. München 1988

Meyer-Abich, Klaus Michael, 'Der Holismus im 20. Jahrhundert'. In *Klassiker der Naturphilosophie. Von den Vorsokratikern bis zur Kopenhagener Schule*, ed. Gernot Bohme, pp. 313-29. Munchen 1989

Meyer-Abich, Klaus Michael, 'Winners and Losers'. In *Options for Controlling Atmospheric CO_2 Accumulation*, ed. G.I.

Pearman, pp. 573-601. New York 1992

Montesquieu, *The Spirit of The Laws* (1748), trans. and ed. A.M. Cohler, B.C. Miller and H.S. Stone. Cambridge 1989

Novalis, *Schriften*, ed. Paul Kluckholm and Richard Samuel (5 vols.). Stuttgart, 1960

Oviedo, Gonzalo Fernández de, *Historia general y natural de las Indias*, Vol. 1. Madrid 1959

Parry, M.L./Carter, T.R./Konjin, N.T. (eds.), *The impact of climatic variations on agriculture*. Vol. I: *Assessment in cool, temperate, and cold regions*. Vol. II: *Assessment in semi-arid regions*. Dordrecht/Boston/London (IIASA-UNEP) 1988

Picht, Georg, 'Der Begriff der Verantwortung' (1967). In *Wahrheit. Vernunft. Verantwortung. Philosophische Studien*, pp. 318-42. Stuttgart 1969,

Rahner, Karl/Vorgrimler, Herbert, *Kleines Konzilskompendium*. Freiburg i. B. 1968

Sahagún, Bernardino de, *Historia general de las cosas de Nueva España*, ed. A.M. Garibay, 5th edn. Mexico City 1982

Saladin, Peter, *Verantwortung als Staatsprinzip. Ein neuer Schlussel zur Lehre vom modernen Rechtsstaat*. Bern/Stuttgart 1984

Scherhorn, Gerhard u.a., *Kausalitätsorientierungen und konsumrelevante Einstellungen*. Stuttgart-Hohenheim, Dec. 1988

Schiller, Friedrich von, 'Ueber naive und sentimentalische Dichtung'. In: *Schillers Werke*, Nationalausgabe (NA) vol. 20. Weimar 1962

Schipperges, Heinrich, 'Die Medizin im Panorama der letzten hundert Jahre. Der Versuch einer Bilanz'. In *mannheimer forum 84/85*. Mannheim 1984/85

Schweitzer, Albert, *Kultur und Ethik* (1923). In *Gesammelte Werke* (5 vols., vol. 2). Munchen 1974

Sitter, Beat, 'Wie läßt sich ökologische Gerechtigkeit denken?' In *Zeitschrift für Evangelische Ethik* 31, (1987) pp. 271-95

Stahl, Friedrich J., *Die Philosophie des Rechts*, Vol. II: *Rechts und Staatslehre auf der Grundlage der christlichen Weltanschauung*, 5th edn. Tübingen 1878

Steiger, Heinhard, *Mensch und Umwelt – Zur Frage der Einführung eines Umweltgrundrechts.* Berlin 1975

Stone, Christopher, *Should Trees have Standing? Towards Legal Rights for Natural Objects* (1972). Los Altos, 1974

Ueberhorst, Reinhard, 'Normativer Diskurs und technologische Entwicklung – Juristische Fiktionen und Noch-nicht-Beiträge'. In *Recht und Technik im Spannungsfeld der Kernenergiekontroverse*, ed. A. Roßnagel. pp. 244-58. Opladen 1984

Uexküll, Jakob von, 'Die Umrisse einer kommenden Weltanschauung'. In *Die neue Rundschau* 18, (1907), pp. 641-61

Uexküll, Jakob von, Umwelt und Innenwelt der Tiere (1909), 2nd edn. Berlin 1921

Uexküll, Jakob von/Kriszat, G., *Streifzüge durch die Umwelten von Tieren und Menschen. Ein Bilderbuch unsichtbarer Welten* (1934). Hamburg 1956

Uexküll, Jakob von, *Bedeutungslehre* (1940). Hamburg 1956

Vogel, Hans-Jochen, 'Eigentumsverfassung – Kontinuität und Wandlung'. In *Politik und Kultur* 3, (1976), pp. 16-30

Vogel, Hans-Jochen, Rede auf dem Außerordentlichen SPD-Bundesparteitag vom 14. Jun 1987

Weizsäcker, Victor von, 'Stücke einer medizinischen Anthropologie. Die Schmerzen' (1926). In *Gesammelte Schriften* vol.5: *Der Arzt und der Kranke. Stücke einer medizinischen Anthropologie*, ed. P. Achilles, pp. 27-47. Frankfurt a.M. 1987

Wilson, Edward O., *Sociobiology: The New Synthesis. Cambridge MA, 1975*

Wolff, Martin/Raiser, Ludwig, *Sachenrecht*, 10th edn. Tubingen 1957